Duty, Honor, Country
The Life of Arthur MacArthur, Jr.

A.K. Brackob

Duty, Honor, Country
The Life of Arthur MacArthur, Jr.

VITA HISTRIA

Vita Histria

Las Vegas ◊ Oxford ◊ Palm Beach

Published in the United States of America by
Histria Books, a division of Histria LLC
7181 N. Hualapai Way, Suite 130-86
Las Vegas, NV 89166 USA
HistriaBooks.com

Vita Histria is an imprint of Histria Books. Titles
published under the imprints of Histria Books are
exclusively distributed worldwide through the Casemate
Group.

Library of Congress Control Number 2020946171

ISBN 978-1-59211-024-7 (hardcover)
ISBN 978-1-59211-116-9 (softbound)

Table of Contents

Preface

On September 15, 1906, Arthur MacArthur Jr. became the twelfth man in the history of the United States Army to be awarded the rank of Lieutenant General, the highest rank in the Army up to that time. This marked the culmination of MacArthur's brilliant military career and included him in an elite group of such outstanding American military leaders as George Washington, Ulysses S. Grant, William Tecumseh Sherman, and Philip H. Sheridan, all of whom had previously had this honor bestowed upon them.[1]

This promotion, by a special act of Congress, bespeaks of the importance of Arthur MacArthur as a figure in American history, but, invariably, when the name MacArthur is mentioned today, it is almost immediately associated with his son Douglas. However, Arthur MacArthur is equally deserving of recognition as a great

---

[1] *Milwaukee Sentinel*, 6 September 1912. This source contains a list of all the men who had held the rank of Lieutenant General before MacArthur.

military leader and, in many ways, one cannot fully appreciate the career of his more famous son without understanding the legacy left to him by his father.

The military career of Arthur MacArthur began when he joined the 24th Wisconsin Infantry regiment and participated in several major battles of the Civil War. By the time he was nineteen, Arthur to become commander of his regiment, and he had attained the rank of Lieutenant Colonel. After the war, MacArthur joined the regular Army and served at various outposts on the western frontier, as well as in Washington, D.C. He proved himself to be an adept soldier.

With the outbreak of the Spanish-American War, MacArthur rose to prominence. After the acquisition of the Philippine Islands from Spain at the conclusion of the war, MacArthur played a key role in suppressing the Philippine Insurrection. After ending the rebellion, he helped shape American policy in the Islands while serving as Military Governor from May 1900 until July 1901. MacArthur's distinguished career came to an end as the United States entered a new era in which it became a world power.

MacArthur stood apart from other political and military figures of the time, in that he demonstrated profound respect for the Filipino people. He treated their leader, Emilio Aguinaldo, with deference after his capture by American forces. He understood and appreciated the Filipino people's natural desire for independence. He understood the growing importance of the Pacific to American policy. Unfortunately, the political leaders of his day did not appreciate MacArthur's vision or share his perspectives.

Arthur MacArthur is truly a representative figure of his time. While MacArthur deserves to be remembered for his remarkable service to his country, the study of his life is also critical to a proper understanding of the life of his famous son Douglas. Many scholars who have studied Douglas MacArthur, including D. Clayton James, Carol Morris Petillo, and others, have recognized this.[2] Douglas MacArthur himself recognized the profound influence his father had on his life. Douglas once remarked, "Of all men I have known, my father was the one I most respected and admired."[3]

This book is intended as a biographical sketch of the life of Arthur MacArthur, Jr., to introduce readers to this remarkable man who served his country with dignity and honor. It does not pretend to be a comprehensive biography, but it is my sincere hope that it will help shed light on this important figure in American history. I began

---

[2]Clark Lee and Richard Henschel, *Douglas MacArthur* (New York: Henry Holt and Company, 1952), pp. 13-14. Lee and Henschel draw important connections between Arthur and Douglas, but ignore Arthur MacArthur's life for the most part.

[3]Carol Morris Petillo, *Douglas MacArthur: The Philippine Years* (Bloomington: Indiana University Press, 1981), pp. 251-252.

research on this book as a student at the University of Wisconsin-Green Bay. After reading a book called *Wisconsin in the Civil War,* by Robert W. Wells of the *Milwaukee Journal,* I became fascinated by the story of Wisconsin's "Boy Colonel." I decided to begin researching his fascinating story in hopes of one day publishing a book to commemorate the life of this great American. Since that time, one notable biography, *The General's General: The Life and Times of Arthur MacArthur* by Kenneth Ray Young, has appeared.[4] It is a fine, well-researched, scholarly study that made a significant contribution. However, as over a quarter of a century has passed since its publication, there is still a need for different perspectives on the first General MacArthur. I hope that this book will make a small contribution to this end.

One issue I want to mention at the outset is the change in the spelling of the family name from McArthur to MacArthur shortly after the Civil War. The specific circumstances surrounding the spelling change are unknown, but I hope to shed some light on this matter. To avoid confusion, the spelling MacArthur will be used consistently throughout the text. I will discuss the issue of the spelling change in an appendix.

---

[4]Kenneth Ray Young, *The General's General: The Life and Times of Arthur MacArthur* (Boulder: Westview Press, 1994).

Many people have helped me in different ways with this project and I would like to acknowledge them here: Dr. Craig Lockard, Dr. Jerrold Rodesch, Dr. Paul Abrahams and Dr. Joyce Salisbury of the University of Wisconsin-Green Bay; Dr. Carol Morris Petillo of Boston College; Mr. Thomas Reitz, Director of the Area Research Center at the University of Wisconsin-Green Bay. I am also indebted to the Wisconsin Historical Society, the Milwaukee County Historical Society, the National Archives, and the MacArthur Memorial in Norfolk, Virginia. Last but not least, I would like to express my sincere gratitude to my wife, Dana, for her love and support throughout the years.

A.K. Brackob

The MacArthur Family

"He made a very profound impression on me; he
wakened in me the first spark of martial ardor that I ever
had, and it has been burning more or less ever since."[5]

— *Arthur MacArthur Jr.*

A n old Scottish proverb says, "There is nothing older than the hills, unless MacArthur and the Devil."[6] The ancestry of the MacArthur family can be traced back to the Atairs of Scotland in the Middle Ages. The Atairs were the head branch of the powerful

---

[5]*The MacArthurs of Milwaukee* (Milwaukee: Milwaukee County Historical Society, 1979), p. 22. This source provides much useful information about the MacArthurs, but lacks documentation and, therefore, must be approached with caution. The quotation is from a speech given by MacArthur in 1910, which is reproduced in this source.

[6]Mary Gates Muggah and Paul H. Raihle, *The MacArthur Story* (Chippewa Falls: Chippewa Falls Book Agency, 1945), p. 12. This highly dramatized source completely lacks documentation and should be approached with caution.

Campbell clan until the reign of James I of Scotland when their chief, John MacArthur, was beheaded at Inverness in 1427, and the King deprived the Atairs of their chieftainship and their territorial possessions. After the demise of the Atairs, a rival clan, the Argyles, became the Chiefs of the Campbell clan.[7] The MacArthurs, however, continued to be a force in Scotland.

Four relatives of Arthur MacArthur Sr. participated in the battle of Culloden on April 16, 1746, in which the Stuarts were defeated in their final attempt to regain the Scottish and English crowns.[8] Two of the MacArthurs who participated in the battle were killed, and the other two escaped. One went to Australia, where the MacArthurs became a wealthy and prominent family.[9]

---

[7]G.T. Ridlon Sr., *Saco Valley Settlements and Families* (Portland, ME: Lakeside Press, 1895), pp. 896-897. Ridlon gives a brief history of the MacArthurs in Scotland. No direct connection is drawn to Judge MacArthur and his family, but the connection is established in a letter from Arthur McArthur to Arthur McArthur dated 28 October 1843 contained in *Papers of Lieutenant-General Arthur MacArthur*, RG-20, MacArthur Archives, Norfolk, VA. This collection will hereafter be referred to as RG 2O, MacArthur Archives. Lee and Henschel, p. 11 claims that Douglas MacArthur was a descendant of Charlemagne, but there is no evidence to support this assertion.

[8]*The Evening Wisconsin*, 27 August 1896; and William L. Langer, ed., *An Encyclopedia of World History* (Boston: Houghton Mifflin Co., 1948), p. 435.

[9]*The Evening Wisconsin*, 27 August 1896.

Arthur MacArthur Sr., the father of Arthur MacArthur Jr., was born in Glasgow, Scotland on January 26, 1817.[10] Arthur MacArthur Sr. had been named for his father Arthur as the family tradition was to name the firstborn son Arthur. The name MacArthur literally means son of Arthur.[11] Ten days before the birth of Arthur Sr., his father and one-year-old sister died[12] probably as the result of some disease. This left Arthur Sr. as the only child of his widowed mother, Sarah. Sarah MacArthur's maiden name had also been MacArthur, leading Arthur Sr., who took great pride in his Scottish heritage, later to proclaim proudly, "I am a double distilled MacArthur."[13]

In 1824, Sarah MacArthur married Alexander Meggett in Glasgow. The promise of a better material future lured the couple, together with young Arthur, Sarah's mother, her two sisters, and her brother to the United States in

---

[10]"Arthur McArthur to Arthur McArthur," 26 October 1843 in RG-20, *MacArthur Archives*; and Robert G. Carroon, "The Judge and the General" in *MacArthurs of Milwaukee*, p. 2; and Ellis Baker Usher, *Wisconsin: Its Story and Biography 1848-1913*, Vol. VII (New York: Lewis Publishing Co., 1914), p. 1837. Several sources say that Arthur MacArthur Sr. was born in 1815, but his own correspondence unequivocally states that he was born in 1817.

[11]*MacArthurs of Milwaukee*, p. 49; and Lee and Henschel, *Douglas MacArthur*, p. 12. This tradition dates back several hundred years.

[12]"Arthur McArthur to Arthur McArthur," 10 October 1863 in RG 20 *MacArthur Archives*.

[13]Ibid.

1828. They first landed at New York and, shortly after, settled in Uxbridge, Massachusetts, perhaps attracted by the employment opportunities offered by the town's vibrant textile manufacturing industry. They lived there for several years.[14]

Despite having to adjust to life in a new country, Arthur Sr.'s boyhood appears to have been relatively secure and his relationship with his stepfather, about whom very little information is known, was apparently quite good. Speaking of Alexander Meggett, Arthur said, "To him, I am greatly indebted for many favors and assistance."[15] Arthur MacArthur became politically aware at an early age and developed strong opinions. Early in his life, he became a member of the Democratic Party. During these early years in the United States, Arthur also decided to become an attorney.[16]

Arthur MacArthur prepared for college by attending Uxbridge and Amherst academies.[17] The MacArthurs had little money, and the family's financial situation worsened

---

[14]Ibid. Several sources say that Arthur Sr. immigrated to the United States in 1825, but his correspondence indicates that it was 1828.

[15]Ibid.

[16]Ibid.

[17]Conklin Mann, "Some Ancestral Lines of General Douglas MacArthur" in *New York Genealogical and Biographical Record*, 73 (July, 1942), p. 171.

when Mr. Meggett died.[18] In any event, Arthur obtained his college education and professional training without the financial assistance of his family.

Arthur entered Wesleyan University, a small Methodist college located in Middletown, Connecticut, in 1836. After spending a short time at Wesleyan, Arthur requested a leave of absence from the school, which he was granted.[19] Financial considerations likely prompted his request. In any event, MacArthur's plans to pursue a college education suddenly changed. In August 1837, Arthur MacArthur wrote a letter to Professor Augustus William Smith, who later became President of Wesleyan University, requesting that he be withdrawn from the University. MacArthur wrote from Norfolk, Virginia that "circumstances have occurred to alter my purpose of returning to Middletown and which require me to end my connection with your institution."[20]

---

[18]The time of Alexander Meggett's death is inferred from the letter "Arthur McArthur to Arthur McArthur," 28 October 1843 in RG-20, *MacArthur Archives*. At the time of the letter in 1843, Arthur Sr. says that his mother was living with one of her sisters in Rhode Island.

[19]"Arthur McArthur to Professor Augustus Smith," 22 August 1837 in RG-20, *MacArthur Archives*.

[20]Ibid.; and "William Manchester to Mrs. Douglas MacArthur," 21 November 1977 in RG-20, *MacArthur Archives*. MacArthur's letter indicates that he had paid his bills at Wesleyan up to that time.

The following year, MacArthur moved to New York City, where he began to study law. Three years later, in 1841, he was admitted to the New York Bar Association. While studying law in New York City, MacArthur met a black-eyed Yankee girl from Springfield named Aurelia Belcher. After his admission to the Bar, Arthur was now ready to establish a family and the couple married. MacArthur practiced law in New York until February 1842 when Aurelia and her friends persuaded him to move his practice to Springfield, Massachusetts.[21]

Aurelia Belcher was the daughter of Benjamin Barney Belcher and his wife, Olive. Benjamin Belcher was a manufacturer in Chicopee Falls, Massachusetts, a suburb of Springfield.[22] Through Arthur MacArthur's marriage to Aurelia Belcher, Douglas MacArthur would be related to

---

[21]"Arthur McArthur to Arthur McArthur," in RG-2O, *MacArthur Archives.* The year 1841 for MacArthur's marriage to Aurelia Belcher is based on this letter, which indicates that MacArthur had been married for a couple of years preceding its writing. Other sources give the date of their marriage as 1844. Mann states that MacArthur was married briefly to a woman named Zelia before he married Aurelia. He is probably referring to MacArthur's second wife, Zolia Hodges, who Arthur married in 1868, four year's after Aurelia's death. Thus, Aurelia was Arthur Sr.'s first wife.

[22]Mann, p. 172.

both Winston Churchill and Franklin D. Roosevelt.[23] While they were living in Chicopee Falls, on June 2, 1845, the first of two sons was born to Arthur and Aurelia MacArthur. Following the family tradition, he was named Arthur.

During his life in Chicopee Falls, Arthur MacArthur Sr. was an active member of the community. He became the Public Administrator of Hampden County and also served as Judge Advocate General for the Western Military District of Massachusetts.[24] Mrs. MacArthur remained at home to raise young Arthur.

During the late 1840s, the newly formed state of Wisconsin was a land of opportunity for ambitious young lawyers like Arthur MacArthur, so, in 1849, he closed his law practice in Springfield and moved his family and his practice to the rapidly growing city of Milwaukee on the shores of Lake Michigan. Milwaukee had a population of about 20,000 people in 1849, and by 1860, the city had

---

[23]Lee and Henschel, p. 11; and William Manchester, *American Caesar: Douglas MacArthur, 1880-1964* (Boston: Little, Brown and Co., 1978), p. 17.

[24]Douglas MacArthur, *Reminiscences* (New York: McGraw-Hill Book Co., 1964), p. 4; and D. Clayton James, *The Years of MacArthur*, Vol. I, 1880-1941 (Boston: Houghton Mifflin Co., 1970), p. 8. Carroon, "The Judge and the General," p. 2, and Mann, p. 171 both indicate that Arthur maintained his law practice in New York City after he moved to Springfield. This seems unlikely and is not substantiated.

grown to 71,440.[25] In 1850, the MacArthurs were boarding
on Osborn Street, in Milwaukee's first ward, amidst the
small but well-organized Scottish population estimated to
be 339 at that time.[26] Arthur MacArthur quickly became
successful in his law practice.

The Scottish community in Milwaukee had played an
active role in local society since the first Scotch Relief
Meeting was held on March 22, 1847. That meeting had
been organized by Alexander Mitchell, a Scotsman and
leading businessman and financier in Wisconsin, to raise
money to assist the victims suffering from the famine in
the Scottish highlands during 1846 and 1847.[27]
Milwaukee's Scottish community was not isolated in the
way the German community, which made up the largest
segment of Milwaukee's population, tended to be. The
Scottish community was quite small, representing less
than two percent of the total population, and its leaders
were well-integrated into the larger Milwaukee society.

---

[25]James, p. 12. James incorrectly identifies Milwaukee as the State
Capitol.

[26]Robert G. Carroon, "Scotsmen in Old Milwaukee, 1810-1860," in
Historical Messenger of the Milwaukee County Historical Center, 25
(March, 1969), p. 26. This source is hereafter cited as Carroon,
"Scotsmen."

[27]Carroon, "Scotsmen", p. 24.

For most Scotsmen, ethnic considerations were an embellishment to their daily activities and nothing more.[28]

An outgoing and gregarious personality, Arthur MacArthur Sr. quickly became a prominent member of the Scottish community and Milwaukee society as a whole. In 1850, MacArthur was selected to deliver an address on the fourth anniversary of the Right Worthy Grand Lodge of Wisconsin, a professional organization.[29] The fact that MacArthur was chosen to deliver this address is an indication of the prominence he had gained after only one year in the city. Certainly, the rapid growth experienced by Milwaukee at that time allowed for a great deal of social mobility which benefitted MacArthur.

On January 21, 1851, an invitation was issued and published in the *Milwaukee Sentinel*, calling on all Scotsmen to attend a dinner commemorating the birth of Scottish poet Robert Burns. The event served as an occasion to organize the Scottish community in the city, something that would prove beneficial to MacArthur as he began to establish himself in his new hometown. The dinner took

---

[28]Kathleen Neils Conzen, *Immigrant Milwaukee, 1836-1860: Accommodation and Community in a Frontier City* (Cambridge: Harvard University Press 1976), p. 170.

[29]Arthur McArthur, *Address of Arthur McArthur Esq. on the 4th Anniversary of the Right Worthy Grand Lodge of Wisconsin* (Milwaukee: Sentinel and Gazette Steam Press Print, 1850). This is a complete text of MacArthur's speech.

place on January 24 at the home of Ben Belden on Spring Street. Approximately fifty people attended the banquet presided over by Arthur MacArthur, Sr. This was the first of the annual Burns dinners that became a fixture in Milwaukee society.[30]

Along with his rise to prominence in Milwaukee social circles, Arthur Sr.'s political ambitions awakened. Later that same year, MacArthur was elected City Attorney of Milwaukee. His election to this post is not surprising given that he had always displayed an interest in political affairs and had held governmental posts when he resided in Chicopee Falls, where he served as a public administrator for Hampden County. His election reflects the prominence that Arthur MacArthur had attained in Milwaukee society after less than two years in the city. It is also evidence of the integration of Scotsmen into the Milwaukee community generally during this time.

On September 20, 1853, a second son was born to Arthur and Aurelia MacArthur. They named the boy Frank.[31] The age difference of eight years and later circumstances prohibited a close relationship from developing between Arthur Jr. and his younger brother.

Successful in his role as City Attorney, and blessed with an outgoing and charming personality, Arthur

---

[30]Carroon, "Scotsman", p. 30.

[31]Mann, p. 172.

MacArthur Sr. continued his rise to prominence. By 1855, he had earned a statewide reputation. Arthur had been active in Democratic Party politics for most of his adult life and, at the nominating convention, the delegates selected him as the party's candidate for Lieutenant Governor that year.

The Democrats faced a difficult election in 1855. They re-nominated incumbent Governor William A. Barstow, whose administration had been plagued by scandal.[32] Having established a reputation for integrity, the Democrats had selected MacArthur in an effort to revitalize the Democratic ticket. The incumbent Democrats faced a stiff challenge from the newly formed Republican Party that had nominated Coles Bashford as its candidate for Governor.

The election took place on November 6, 1855. The vote tallies revealed a close battle in the Governor's race. The results of the county by county canvass indicated that Bashford had received 35,872 votes to Barstow's 35,523, giving the Republican candidate a margin of victory of 349

---

[32]Edward M. Hunter, "Civil Life, Services and Character of William A. Barstow" in Lyman Copeland Draper, ed., *Collections of the State Historical Society of Wisconsin*, Vol. VI (Madison: State Historical Society of Wisconsin, 1908), p. 103. Hunter provides an apologetic view of Barstow.

votes.[33] MacArthur won election as Lieutenant Governor by a wide margin, running well-ahead of the rest of the Democratic ticket. The ease of MacArthur's election demonstrates the validity of the Democrats' reasoning that he could draw support to the ailing Barstow administration.

On December 17, 1855, the State Board of Canvass, which was responsible for certifying the final results, came out with revised figures that indicated that Barstow had received 36,355 votes to 36,198 votes for Bashford. These revised figures made Bashford the winner of the gubernatorial election by 157 votes.[34] This created a great deal of controversy, with Republicans charging that there had been fraud in the election.

Governor Barstow called out the militia to keep order as he and MacArthur were inaugurated on January 7, 1856. On that same day, the Supreme Court of the State of Wisconsin announced that it would examine charges of voting fraud leveled by Bashford and the Republicans against Barstow.[35] Over the next several months, tensions grew in Madison, the State Capitol. Ironically, one of the leading state Democrats, Attorney Edward Ryan,

---

[33]Fred L. Holmes, Ed., *Wisconsin: Stability, Progress, Beauty, Vol. II* (Chicago: Lewis Publishing Co., 1946), p. 23.

[34]Holmes, p. 23.

[35]Holmes, p. 25; and James, p. 9.

represented the Republicans before the Supreme Court. During the deliberations, it was discovered that unanimous votes for Barstow were reported from two fictional townships in Chippewa County, Bridge Creek and Spring Grove.[36] When this became public, Barstow, acting on the advice of counsel, resigned as Governor.

In accordance with the State Constitution, Arthur MacArthur, Sr. succeeded Barstow as Governor on March 21, 1856.[37] MacArthur served as Governor for four days until the Supreme Court certified Bashford as the legitimate winner of the election.[38] During his short tenure as Governor, MacArthur grappled with the difficult decision of whether to accept the Court's jurisdiction in this matter or to attempt to hold the office of Governor. MacArthur was encouraged by many supporters and Democratic Party officials to keep the office on the basis that his own election had been legitimate, as had been his succession to the Governor's office. They further argued that the Court did not have jurisdiction in the case and the results certified by the State Board of Canvass were final.

---

[36]Muggah and Raihle, p. 11.

[37]John G. Gregory, *History of Milwaukee, Vol. II* (Chicago: S.J. Clarke Publishing Co., 1931), p. 926; and James, p. 9.

[38]Hunter, p.105

It was also pointed out that MacArthur would have the militia to back him up should he chose to retain the office.[39]

MacArthur weighed his options carefully before being visited by Bashford and Attorney Edward Ryan at the State Capitol. Although he believed that the election was a political rather than a judicial matter, Bashford's allusion to the potential use of force concerned him. So when the Governor-elect arrived, MacArthur greeted Bashford and informed him of his decision, "I yield to a constructive force — the Supreme Court. Best Wishes."[40] MacArthur thus relinquished the office of Governor to Bashford and resumed his duties as Lieutenant Governor.[41] MacArthur received criticism from some Democrats for his decision,[42] but it appears to have had very little negative impact on his political career. MacArthur's legal training and respect for the judicial system certainly informed his decision to yield to the office of Governor.

---

[39]Lee and Henschel, p. 12; and Muggah and Raihle, p. 13. Muggah and Raihle present a highly dramatic and undocumented account of MacArthur's decision in chapter 1, pp. 11-15.

[40]Richard N. Current, *The History of Wisconsin II: The Civil War Era, 1848-1873* (Madison, State Historical Society of Wisconsin, 1976), pp. 229-230; *Evening Wisconsin*, August 27, 1896; and Muggah and Raihle, p. 14.

[41]Usher, p. 1838; and Hunter, p. 105.

[42]Muggah and Raihle, p. 15.

As a Democratic Lieutenant Governor serving in a Republican administration, MacArthur had a minimal role outside of performing his constitutionally specified duty of presiding over the Senate when it was in session. This allowed him to continue to devote time to his law practice in Milwaukee where he continued to reside. MacArthur's disassociation from the Bashford administration proved to be politically beneficial. Bashford's administration would be even more scandal-ridden than the administration of his predecessor, Barstow.[43]

Arthur MacArthur remained unaffected by both the election scandal that had forced the resignation of Governor Barstow and the scandals of the Bashford administration. While still serving as Lieutenant Governor in 1857, he was elected Judge of the Circuit Court of Wisconsin's second judicial district, which included Milwaukee.[44] This position was better suited to MacArthur's legal interests, and, after two very difficult years, he gladly left State government at the end of his term.

As a Judge, MacArthur was described as "a well-informed, genial, kindly gentleman and an excellent judge when he applied himself to his task. It was said of him that he did not think it well to work too hard. He was a

---

[43]James, p. 9.

[44]Gregory, p. 926; and Manchester, p. 18.

Scotchman of the deepest dye and presided at all Scotch banquets with great efficiency, at which he took delight and a little Scotch whisky. Once, it was said of him that he should be elected perpetual president of festive occasions."[45] This is perhaps part of the reason for Mac-Arthur's success as a politician. He did not take

Arthur MacArthur, Sr.

himself or his work too seriously, and although he certainly enjoyed social functions, he was highly intelligent and diligent in his work.

His good nature and outgoing personality made MacArthur a very popular man. MacArthur's jovial nature is further revealed in a letter he wrote to his friend Charles D. Robinson, editor of the *Green Bay Advocate*: "So look at the bench, where injustice I clench. But when things are done, let us have lots of fun. Right here in Milwaukee, without being naughty, and so without water, I'm Arthur MacArthur."[46]

---

[45]Gregory, p. 932. The author does not identify whom he is quoting.

[46]"Arthur McArthur to Charles D. Robinson," 17 October 1863 in Charles D. Robinson Papers, SC 229, State Historical Society of

MacArthur's continued his involvement in Milwaukee's Scottish community and took great pleasure in social affairs. On the centennial of the birth of the Scottish poet Robert Burns on January 25, 1859, the St. Andrew's Society was formed at the annual Burn's dinner.[47] The St. Andrew's Society was created to combine the charitable and social functions of the Scottish community. The motto, "Relieve the distressed" was adopted at the banquet attended by approximately sixty people. The officers elected at this meeting included Alexander Mitchell as President and Arthur MacArthur as first Vice-President.[48] As was customary, MacArthur presided at the banquet and delivered one of the

---

Wisconsin. This collection is hereafter cited as Robinson Papers, SHSW.

[47]*The Centennial Anniversary of the Birthday of Robert Burns as Commemorated by his Countrymen in the City of Milwaukee, Wisconsin, January 25, 1859* (Milwaukee: Daily News Book and Job Steam Printing Establishment, 1859). This is the proceedings of the banquet at which the St. Andrew's Society was founded. It is hereafter cited as *Centennial Anniversary of the Birthday of Robert Burns.* For additional information see St. Andrew's Society Collection, Milwaukee County Historical Society, hereafter cited as St. Andrew's, MCHS.

[48]Carroon,"Scotsmen", p. 30; and *History of Milwaukee, Wisconsin, Vol. I* (Chicago: The Western Historical Co., 1881), p. 576; and *Centennial Anniversary of the Birthday of Robert Burns,* p. 6, for results of the election and other officers elected.

speeches.[49] Arthur MacArthur remained active in the St. Andrew's Society throughout his life in Milwaukee and served as its President from 1860 to 1862 and again from 1863 to 1866.[50] The purpose of the St. Andrew's Society would later be defined as "to keep alive the memory of Scotland, her manners and customs, literature and games, and to afford relief to her children and descendants when in need."[51]

Arthur MacArthur, Jr. grew up in the midst of his father's activities. Occupied most of the time with his political and social functions, Judge MacArthur had little time to spend raising the boy. Mrs. MacArthur was occupied bringing up her younger son Frank. This left young Arthur to grow up in the company afforded by the neighborhood.[52] Early in the 1850s, the MacArthurs had

---

[49]*Centennial Anniversary of the Birthday of Robert Burns*. See pp. 9-13 for MacArthur's speech.

[50]St. Andrew's, MCHS. From 1859 to 1866 the presidency of the organization traded between Mitchell and MacArthur. This reflects the prominent role of these two men in the Scottish community.

[51]*History of Milwaukee, Wisconsin, Vol. 1*, p. 567. The Society adopted this definition of purpose in 1867.

[52]Charles King Papers, Micro A79, State Historical Society of Wisconsin King's recollection of MacArthur's boyhood is not flawless as he states that MacArthur grew up motherless. This is not so as Aurelia lived until 1864. These recollections of MacArthur's boyhood by King can also be found in *MacArthurs of Milwaukee*, pp. 16-20.

taken up residence at 448 (now 762 N.) Van Buren Street,[53] located in the seventh ward on Milwaukee's east side. There was a great deal of rivalry at this time between the boys of the seventh ward and their fellow east siders from the first and third wards, often resulting in fights between these groups.[54]

The next door neighbors of the MacArthurs were the Kings, who resided at the corner of Mason and Van Buren streets. Rufus King, the editor of the *Milwaukee Sentinel*, was a prominent figure in Milwaukee society. His grandfather of the same name was a signer of the United States Constitution. His son, Charles, would become one of Arthur Jr.'s closest friends and would remain so throughout his life. The boys of the seventh ward, including Arthur MacArthur Jr. and Charles King, would gather at the corner of Mason and Van Buren street, in front of the King home, each day at nightfall. Arthur Jr. was a small boy and one of the youngest members of this group, which came to be known as the King's Corner gang.[55]

Arthur Jr. and his friends attended school at what they referred to as the Milwaukee University, a public school where boys from ages ten to sixteen prepared for business

---

[53]Carroon, "The Judge and the General," p. 9.

[54]Charles King Papers, SHSW.

[55]Ibid.

or college.[56] As a boy, Arthur took very little interest in his education. Charles King later recollected, "MacArthur could not be made to learn his lesson, especially catechism."[57] Arthur's interests were chiefly confined to outdoor activities, such as a game of pom-pom-pull-away. Though MacArthur was one of the youngest members of the King's Corner gang, he is said to have displayed leadership in the games and activities of the boys.

Perhaps feeling a need to compensate for his small size and youth, MacArthur tried extra hard to prove himself an equal of the older boys. Doing so gave him a feeling of belonging to the group and provided a sense of security to the young MacArthur. The neighborhood mothers saw the boys of the King's Corner gang as idlers and triflers and generally a nuisance to the neighborhood. Eventually, because of such parental concerns, Charles King was sent away to school in New York.[58]

An important event in Arthur MacArthur Jr.'s childhood occurred in 1857 when Charles Cotton, a former

---

[56]*Milwaukee Journal*, 6 September 1912.

[57]Charles King Papers, SHSW. James, p. 12, Lee and Henschel, p. 14 and others all state that MacArthur was very studious and an ardent reader. This assumption seems to be based on MacArthur's later life and is unsubstantiated by the evidence of his childhood. MacArthur took very little interest in reading and studying as a young boy growing up in Milwaukee.

[58]Charles King Papers, SHSW.

member of the King's Corner gang, returned home on furlough from the Naval Academy dressed in his midshipman's uniform. Cotton later went on to become an Admiral in the Navy. As MacArthur recalled in later years, "He made a very profound impression on me; he wakened in me the first spark of martial ardor that I ever had, and it has been burning more or less ever since."[59] Aside from MacArthur and Cotton, several members of the King's Corner gang went on to achieve some prominence, including King, who became a General, James K. Cogswell, who became an Admiral in the Navy[60] and James G. Flanders, who became a prominent attorney and a leader in Wisconsin's Progressive movement.[61]

Arthur decided early on to pursue a military career. Cotton's homecoming provoked young Arthur to plead with his father to let him become a midshipman.[62] Perhaps MacArthur was intent upon a military career because it seemed to provide the same type of fraternal, organized structure that the King's Corner gang had offered him. Surely, Cotton's uniform represented a sense of belonging that seemed so important for young Arthur's emotional security.

---

[59]*MacArthurs of Milwaukee*, p. 22.

[60]Charles King Papers, SHSW.

[61]James, p. 12.

[62]Lee and Henschel, p. 14.

With the election of Abraham Lincoln as President in 1860, the rift between north and south that had long plagued the young nation devolved into secession. On April 12, 1861, the Confederates fired upon Fort Sumter in South Carolina, and it was clear that war was at hand. For young Arthur, the Civil War provided the opportunity to pursue the military career he had long desired. The War would forever change the history of the United States and the lives of all those who survived it. The Civil War provided Arthur MacArthur Jr. with opportunities that would otherwise have not opened up to him and impacted the remainder of his life.

Chapter II
A Call to Arms

"Colonel MacArthur on all occasions distinguished himself for gallantry and efficiency as an officer. I can say with truth that Colonel MacArthur has not his superior as an officer in the Army."[63]

— Major General Nathan Kimball

When conflict between the states became inevitable following the election of Abraham Lincoln as the 16th President of the United States in 1860, Judge MacArthur clearly indicated that he favored the preservation of the Union at all costs. A Union meeting was held in Milwaukee on February 4, 1861, to rally people behind the northern cause. Judge MacArthur was one of the keynote speakers.[64] Throughout his adult

---

[63]"Nathan Kimball to E.M. Stanton," 13 April 1865 in Usher, p. 1848.

[64]Carroon, "The Judge and the General," p. 5.

life, Arthur MacArthur Sr. had been a Democrat and actively involved in political matters. Now, the party to which he belonged and had unwaveringly stood by in times of crisis, such as during the Barstow-Bashford election controversy, would be torn apart by the war.

Arthur MacArthur Jr. was not yet sixteen when the War between the States broke out in early 1861, but he was determined to participate in it. Undoubtedly, his father's pro-Union political beliefs, combined with his own desire for a military career, influenced him. The outbreak of the War made the Spring of 1861 an exciting time for the young boy who desperately wanted to become a soldier.

Arthur, Jr. was determined to enlist as a Private in the 1st Wisconsin Infantry then being organized at Camp Scott in Milwaukee under the direction of General John C. Starkweather, but his father refused to give his consent.[65] Judge MacArthur was a friend of General Starkweather and undoubtedly could have secured a place in the regiment for Arthur, despite his youth, had he chosen to do so. Young Arthur persisted in his attempts to enlist. He tried to join the 6th Wisconsin Infantry, but he was rejected on account of his size and youth.[66]

---

[65]*Milwaukee Sentinel*, 6 September 1912.

[66]Major J.A. Watrous, "How the Boy Won: General MacArthur's First Victory" in *Saturday Evening Post*, 172 (February 24, 1900), p. 770.

Arthur Sr. realized that he had to do something to stop his overeager son from enlisting in the Army. The Judge persuaded the boy to study in a private military academy in Milwaukee for a year. To ensure that he did so, Judge MacArthur also employed a private detective to watch the boy so that he would not join some regiment leaving for the front.[67] Young Arthur accepted this arrangement with great reluctance. Like many others during this period of the War, he felt it would be a short engagement and that waiting a year might cause him to miss the entire conflict and, with that, his chance for military glory. His father, however, gave the boy little choice. Indeed, Judge MacArthur hoped that diverting his son to a military academy would cause him to miss participating in the War.

Arthur's determination to pursue a military career is not surprising. His father, who took great pride in the family's Scottish heritage, undoubtedly regaled him with tales of the famous deeds of the MacArthurs as warriors in Scotland. It has been suggested that young Arthur's hero was Abraham Lincoln and that he was vehemently opposed to slavery and that these factors, combined with a desire to preserve the Union, motivated him to join the

---

[67]Usher, p. 1840; and Muggah and Raihle, p. 16; and MacArthur, p. 6; and James, p. 12. What Academy MacArthur studied at is unknown.

Union Army.[68] There is no evidence, however, that political views played any role in Arthur's decision to become a soldier. It is also unlikely that the boy had any particular affection for Lincoln. In 1860, Judge MacArthur was a Democrat and a supporter of the party's presidential candidate, Stephen Douglas. The Judge, like most other War Democrats, was not opposed to slavery. What prompted Judge MacArthur to support the War effort was a firm belief in the preservation of the Union at all costs. There is no evidence to suggest that young Arthur held any political beliefs that substantially differed from this of his father. Arthur Jr. seems to have had little interest in politics at this time, and his desire to become a soldier should not be construed as reflecting any particular ideology.

During his time at the military academy, Arthur worked hard and was very successful.[69] The boy's sudden academic success must have come as a surprise to his father. With the clear goal of a military career in mind, Arthur felt he had found a purpose and devoted all of his energies toward his studies. The boy was determined to succeed in school. He knew that if he failed to do so Judge MacArthur would have additional cause to deny him permission to pursue the military career he desired.

---

[68]MacArthur, p. 6; and Usher, p. 1840.

[69]MacArthur, p. 6.

Arthur was so successful that it was recommended that he attend West Point. Judge MacArthur certainly would have favored this option as it seemed less and less likely that there would be a quick end to the war. Judge MacArthur's enthusiasm for the idea that Arthur attend West Point is evidenced by the fact that he used his political connections to try to obtain an appointment to the military academy for his son, despite the fact that the two appointments from Wisconsin were already filled. One of these appointments had gone to Arthur's friend Charles King.

Judge MacArthur arranged for young Arthur to accompany Wisconsin Senator James R. Doolittle to Washington, D.C. to see if the boy could get an appointment from President Lincoln to attend West Point that year. The Judge wrote to President Lincoln:

Sir,

Accompanying this letter will be one from Governor Saloman introducing my son Arthur McArthur, Jr., and asking you to appoint him as a cadet to the National Military School at West Point.

The lad will reach his seventeenth year next June, and a desire to go into the military service of the country has become the absorbing object of his very existence. This is not a light or sudden impression with him, for he has been dwelling upon it or the Navy for the last two years, so that it has become the fixed heart of his inclination. My affection and interest in his welfare leave me no alternative but to promote his desire...

Like his father, he is intensely patriotic and detests treason as much as he does murder or arson. Indeed, I have no hesitation in pledging myself for his good behavior and I feel sure that he would be a brave and useful officer.[70]

Although impressed with the young man, Lincoln had to send young Arthur back to Milwaukee as his appointments for that year had already been decided. The boy did receive a promise of an appointment for the following year,[71] but this held little interest for him.

The fact that Arthur did not wait an additional year to attend West Point demonstrates the lukewarm enthusiasm he had for the idea all along. He sensed that his moment in history was at hand. West Point, while assuring him of a military career, would certainly interfere with his chance for military glory which could only be won on the battlefield. The idea of waiting another year for an

---

[70]"Arthur McArthur to Abraham Lincoln, May 13, 1862," in Lt. Gen. A. MacArthur, Correspondence and Records, War Department, 1862-1944, National Archives, Microcopy 1064, Roll 277. Hereafter cited at MacArthur Correspondence, National Archives.

[71]Carroon, "The Judge and the General", p. 5; and MacArthur, p. 6; and Manchester, p. 15; and James, p. 11.

appointment to West Point, however, certainly appealed to Judge MacArthur, who understandably would have preferred to keep his eldest son far from the bloody battlefields.

The time had finally come when the father would have to relent and allow his son to enlist. Young Arthur was not particular about how he got to the front, only that he got there. Judge MacArthur finally gave his consent, albeit reluctantly, for Arthur to enlist, but he was not going to let his son haphazardly go off with any regiment that allowed the boy to sign up. Having decided that Arthur could go off to war, the Judge used his extensive political influence in the state and went to see Governor Edward R. Salomon about an appointment for his son.

In Madison, the Judge secured an appointment for young Arthur as First Lieutenant and Adjutant of the 24th Wisconsin Infantry then being organized in Milwaukee.[72] When Judge MacArthur returned to Milwaukee and presented his son with an envelope that read "Arthur MacArthur – Adjutant," the boy thought that his father had himself enlisted so that he could watch over him. Arthur Jr. was both surprised and delighted to find out that the commission contained in the envelope was for him and not his father.[73] Arthur MacArthur Jr. received his

---

[72]Watrous, p. 770.

[73]Ibid.

commission as First Lieutenant and Adjutant of the 24th Wisconsin Infantry on August 4, 1862.[74]

The 24th Wisconsin Volunteer Infantry regiment arose out of the first war meeting held in Milwaukee on April 15, 1861, to stimulate recruiting as the North mobilized for the War. On July 23, 1862, the Milwaukee Chamber of Commerce, then known as the Milwaukee Merchant's Association, committed $2,000 toward the promotion of enlistments in the 24th Wisconsin regiment. An additional $10,000 was later raised through private funding.[75] The regiment's recruiting officers were William H. Eldred and Howard Greene.[76] The 24th Wisconsin was organized at Camp Sigel in Milwaukee during August under the direction of Colonel Charles H. Larabee. The regiment was formally mustered into service on August 21, 1862.[77] Initially nicknamed the "Milwaukee Tigers",[78] the regiment later came to be known simply as the

---

[74]"In Memoriam Companion Arthur MacArthur Lieutenant General U.S.A." No. 506 in *Circulars, 447-545, Military Order of the Loyal Legion of the United States, Commandery of Wisconsin, 1909-1916.* Hereafter, this will be cited as *Circulars.*

[75]*Milwaukee Sentinel,* 6 September 1912.

[76]*Milwaukee Sentinel,* 11 August 1862.

[77]Charles E. Estabrook, ed., *Records and Sketches of Military Organizations* (Madison: State of Wisconsin – Democrat Printing Co., 1914), p. 1&6; and *Milwaukee Sentinel,* 16 June 1865.

[78]*Milwaukee Sentinel,* 11 August 1862.

"Milwaukee Regiment" as it's recruits were largely residents of Milwaukee and neighboring communities.

Young Arthur MacArthur did not receive a warm welcome from the men of the 24th regiment. The Colonel resented the fact that the Governor had sent him a boy to do a man's job,[79] but realizing the extent of Judge MacArthur's influence in Milwaukee and the State, he knew there was very little that he could do about it. The older men of the regiment resented the fact that the boy had been given a commission they did not think he was worthy to hold.

As Adjutant of the regiment, Arthur had to study intensely for his new job because a great deal of responsibility had suddenly been thrust upon his shoulders. The *Milwaukee Sentinel* published Colonel Larabee's order on August 15, 1862 that "All applications for furlough or in regard to any matter affecting the regiment must be addressed to the Adjutant."[80] Arthur's diligent study during the previous year and his determination to prove he could handle this position of responsibility paid off. Arthur learned his new job and handled the responsibilities well.

Still, his first month as Adjutant of the newly formed regiment was not altogether without difficulty. Arthur's

---

[79]*Charles King Papers*, SHSW.

[80]*Milwaukee Sentinel*, 15 August 1862.

first appearance on dress parade could only be characterized as an unmitigated disaster. The young MacArthur's voice cracked as he gave out orders and he appeared clumsy and awkward, arousing laughter and snide comments from the men of his regiment as well as onlookers.[81] This experience deeply upset young Arthur who had worked so hard to gain the respect of the men of his regiment, but he did not let this unpleasant event demoralize him. It only served to further strengthen his resolve to prove that he belonged in the regiment and was worthy of his commission.

This tenacity had characterized the boy throughout his childhood. As a child, Arthur had usually associated with boys several years his elder and he had to work extra hard to gain their acceptance. Failure only served to strengthen Arthur's determination. Arthur told a Captain in the regiment, shortly after his unsuccessful appearance on parade, "I know why I am a soldier and I know that when the actual work of the regiment begins in battle, I will be found doing my duty as well as anyone in this regiment."[82] Young MacArthur was not a quitter and his next appearance on parade in his hometown would be a far

---

[81]*Milwaukee Sentinel*, 6 September 1912; and Muggah and Raihle, p. 17; *Milwaukee Sentinel* and Watrous, p. 770; and *Circulars*.

[82]*Milwaukee Sentinel*, 6 September 1912.

greater success than anyone, except perhaps Arthur himself, could imagine.

On September 5, 1862 the 24th Wisconsin Volunteer Infantry regiment left Milwaukee headed for the front with young Arthur MacArthur as First Lieutenant and Adjutant. The regiment arrived at Jeffersonville, Indiana, across the river from Louisville, Kentucky, two days later, on September 7.[83] The regiment camped here for three days before being sent to Cincinnati, Ohio on September 10. After arriving in Cincinnati, the 24th Wisconsin was sent to Covington, Kentucky, where it remained until September 18. The regiment was then ordered back to Louisville, returning by boat, as the likelihood of a battle in that area of Kentucky began to appear likely.[84]

Arthur's first taste of battle came soon after, as the Union and Confederate forces met in battle at Chaplain Hills (Perryville), Kentucky, on October 8, 1862. Young Arthur took advantage of this first opportunity to prove himself in combat. He made a successful reconnaissance to

---

[83]Henry A. Fant, *Arthur MacArthur and the Philippine Insurrection* (unpublished M.A. Thesis, Mississippi State University, 1963). On page 6, Fant incorrectly states that the 24th went to Illinois for training after leaving Milwaukee on September 5.

[84]*Milwaukee Sentinel*, 16 June 1865. There is no regimental history of the 24th Wisconsin, but this issue of the *Milwaukee Sentinel* contains a concise summary of the regiment's activities, especially useful up to early 1864.

Arthur MacArthur, Jr. during the Civil War

ascertain the position of the Confederate forces.[85] Then, when the Union Army began to retreat in the face of a vigorous attack by Braxton Bragg's rebel forces, the Union center, comprised of General Philip A. Sheridan's division, which included the 24th Wisconsin, held firm in part due to the information that Adjutant MacArthur had provided. The battle ended indecisively, but Sheridan's division had averted a potential catastrophe by halting the Confederate assault. The 24th Wisconsin with its youthful Adjutant distinguished itself in the battle. General Sheridan cited Arthur for "gallantry under fire" and made him a brevet Captain.[86] Arthur MacArthur had proved himself a man and quickly alleviated the resentment of the other members of his regiment.

After the battle of Chaplain Hills, the 24th Wisconsin pursued the Confederate Army southward. The regiment reached Crab Orchard, Kentucky, on October 15 and remained there until October 20. The regiment then engaged in a series of movements until it reached Bowling Green, Kentucky, on the first of November where it remained until November 4 when it was ordered to Edgefield, Tennessee, near Nashville. The 24th Wisconsin reached Edgefield on November 8 and camped there until November 22 when it marched through Nashville to Mill

---

[85]Watrous, p. 771.

[86]Usher, p. 1840; and MacArthur, p. 8; and James, p. 13; and Manchester, p. 15.

Creek, Tennessee. Up to this point, the 24th Wisconsin had done more marching than fighting. This certainly must have frustrated young Arthur who craved further opportunities for glory on the battlefield. The 24th Wisconsin remained at Mill Creek until December 26, 1862, when it received orders to move to Murfreesboro, Tennessee, southeast of Nashville. The regiment arrived on December 30, just as the battle of Murfreesboro (Stone's River) drew near.[87]

At the battle of Murfreesboro, the 24th Wisconsin was commanded by Major Elisha C. Hibbard, as Colonel Larabee had fallen ill, and Lieutenant Colonel Edwin L. Buttrick had resigned the week before. Major Hibbard was assisted by Adjutant MacArthur.[88] The Confederates overwhelmed the right-wing of the Union lines in the attack on December 31. The 24th Wisconsin was among the units to suffer the onslaught of the Confederate attack. Once again, Adjutant MacArthur rose to the occasion. An officer of the regiment later recalled that, as panic and disorder were imminent due to the break in the Union lines, "The Adjutant at once grasped the situation and, being the only mounted officer in sight, for the moment

---

[87]*Milwaukee Sentinel*, 16 June 1865.

[88]Robert W. Wells, *Wisconsin in the Civil War* (Milwaukee: *The Milwaukee Journal*, 1964), p. 49; and *Roster of Wisconsin Volunteers, War of the Rebellion, 1861-1865*, Vol. II (Madison: Democrat Printing Co., State Printers, 1886), p. 256.

assumed command and by his ringing orders and perfect coolness, checked the impending panic, restored confidence, rallied and held the regiment in line until completely flanked, it fell back slowly and in order delivering its fire as it did so."[89] The battle of Murfreesboro ended indecisively, but MacArthur had once again proven himself in a combat situation. After the battle, Major Hibbard wrote, "To the adjutant of the regiment, I am more than indebted for his aid and efficient service rendered during the engagements. I bespeak for him an honorable military career."[90] By this time, MacArthur had certainly put to rest any lingering doubts about his capabilities.

After the battle, the 24th Wisconsin remained in Murfreesboro performing garrison, scouting, and foraging duties until June 24, 1863.[91] In the summer of 1863, Judge MacArthur traveled to Tennessee to visit his son.[92] Mrs. MacArthur and young Frank remained in Milwaukee. The Judge must have been quite proud of his son and his success as a soldier. After Judge MacArthur's visit, the

---

[89]Usher, p. 1841.

[90]*Milwaukee Sentinel*, 6 September 1912.

[91]*Milwaukee Sentinel*, 16 June 1865; and Estabrook, p. 1&6.

[92]Carroon, "The Judge and the General", p. 9. Carroon says Arthur got typhoid fever and returned to Milwaukee with his father. This is incorrect as Arthur returned in September after Judge MacArthur had already returned, sometime prior to August.

regiment took part in a series of minor movements in Tennessee, but it was not engaged in any major battles.[93]

Near the end of the summer, Arthur contracted typhoid fever and returned to Milwaukee, spending the month of September on furlough recuperating.[94] During his absence, the regiment was ordered to Chattanooga, Tennessee, to participate in the Union advance into Georgia. The regiment participated in the battle of Chickamauga on September 19, led by Lieutenant Colonel Theodore S. West. West had replaced Colonel Larabee in command of the regiment after Larabee resigned in August 1863.[95] The first day of the battle of Chickamauga was a stalemate, but on the second day, a Union blunder allowed the Confederates to break the Union lines and forced the Yankees to retreat to Chattanooga.[96] At Chattanooga, the Union Army was immediately put under siege by Bragg's confederate force. Arthur recovered quickly from typhoid fever and hurried back to the front to join his regiment in Chattanooga.

---

[93]*Milwaukee Sentinel*, 16 June 1865; Estabrook, p. 146.

[94]MacArthur, p. 8; and Cartoon, "The Judge and the General", pp. 5, 9.

[95]*Milwaukee Sentinel*, 16 June 1865; and *Roster of Wisconsin Volunteers*, p. 256.

[96]Wells, p. 61.

1863 was a particularly busy year for Judge MacArthur. He was easily elected to a second six-year term as Judge of the 2nd District Circuit Court. It was also a crucial year for the Democratic Party in Wisconsin of which Judge MacArthur was still a prominent member. The War had a devastating effect on the Democratic Party in Wisconsin, as well as throughout the northern states. Democrats were divided into two camps; the War Democrats who favored preservation of the Union and supported the war effort on those grounds, and the Copperheads who opposed the prosecution of the war. This split became especially apparent in the summer of 1863 as the Democrats prepared for the gubernatorial election.

One of the leading forces of the Copperhead movement in Wisconsin was Edward Ryan, who had represented Republican Coles Bashford in his appeal to the Supreme Court eight years earlier. The Democratic convention was held in Madison on August 6, 1863. The Copperheads, led by Ryan, were able to control the convention and put their candidates on the party's ticket for the November election.[97]

This caused a great deal of resentment on behalf of the War Democrats, among them Arthur MacArthur Sr. The

---

[97]Current, pp. 401-413, gives a summary of Wisconsin politics at this time.

War Democrats were led by the editor of the *Green Bay Advocate*, Charles D. Robinson. The War Democrats entertained thoughts of forming a third party and organized their own convention, which they called the Loyal Democratic Convention. The convention was held in Janesville on September 17, 1863, and was attended by leading War Democrats, including Robinson, MacArthur, Matthew H. Carpenter, and Levi Hubbell.[98] The convention did not produce a third party. Rather, the War Democrats agreed to a temporary merger with the Republicans to form the Union ticket for the 1863 election. This course of action had been advocated by Republicans ever since the bitter split in the Democratic ranks had occurred in August.[99] Republicans feared that if War Democrats formed a third party they could conceivably split the pro-Union vote enough to allow the Copperheads to win the election. War Democrats realized this and accepted the Union ticket as the most viable path to stop the Copperheads in the 1863 election.

As part of the Union arrangement, the Republicans appointed Robinson and Carpenter as members of the State Republican Central Committee. They also nominated

---

[98]Robinson Papers, SHSW. This collection contains a complete roster of the approximately forty people who attended the Loyal Democratic Convention in Janesville.

[99]For evidence of this see Robinson Papers, SHSW. Many of the letters in this collection deal with the 1863 election campaign.

one of the chief architects of this temporary union, J.T. Lewis, a former Democrat, who had switched to the Republican Party in 1861, as their candidate for Governor. Lucius Fairchild, a War Democrat and a war hero himself, was nominated as the party's candidate for Secretary of State. This strategy proved successful as Lewis easily won the election. The success of the union of the Republicans and the War Democrats in the election of 1863 is best reflected by the fact that Fairchild, the only Democrat on the Union ticket, ran well ahead of the rest of the ticket.

This break in the ranks of the Democratic Party would be significant for Judge MacArthur. The Union ticket was only intended as a temporary measure to prevent the election of the Copperheads. The following year, the War Democrats split between those who would rejoin the Party and those who became Republicans. Judge MacArthur was among those who changed parties in 1864.[100]

Arthur Jr.'s furlough in September 1863 would be the last time he would see his mother. Aurelia MacArthur died in early 1864,[101] leaving Judge MacArthur to raise ten-year-old Frank. When ·Adjutant MacArthur returned to his regiment in Chattanooga, he was no longer an

---

[100]"Robinson to McArthur, 5 March 1865" in Robinson Papers, SHSW.

[101]Carroon, "The Judge and the General," pp. 3-4, 9; and Mann, p. 172.

inexperienced young boy, but a battle-tested veteran soldier. MacArthur's finest moment, however, was still yet to come.

The Union position at Chattanooga was becoming desperate as the Army had been under siege for nearly two months and lacked supplies. The North's ablest Generals, including Ulysses S. Grant, William T. Sherman, Philip Sheridan, and George Thomas commanded the Union Army at Chattanooga. The Union force of nearly 60,000 men had been attempting to break the Confederate siege of Chattanooga since November 23, but had very little success. The Confederate Army had been able to maintain the siege, with the main point of its line high atop the well-fortified Missionary Ridge.

At 3:30 p.m. on November 25, 1863, General Grant called up Union forces being held in reserve and ordered them to seize the rifle pits at the base of Missionary Ridge.[102] Among the troops ordered to perform this task was the 24th Wisconsin with its youthful Adjutant Arthur MacArthur. The 24th Wisconsin formed a part of the 1st Brigade of the 2nd Division commanded by General Sheridan.[103]

---

[102]Manchester, pp. 13-14.

[103]Captain E.B. Parsons, "Missionary Ridge" in *War Papers Read Before the Commandery of Wisconsin, Military Order of the Loyal Legion*

BATTLE OF MISSIONARY RIDGE

The assault began as the Union forces charged the Confederate rifle pits at the base of Missionary Ridge. In fierce hand to hand combat, the Union soldiers successfully seized the rifle pits. After a brief delay, the men then began to force their way up the ridge.[104] Captain E.B. Parsons of the 24th Wisconsin wrote to his father shortly after the battle, "General Sheridan, who was right

of the United States, Vol. I (Milwaukee: Burdick, Armitage and Allen, 1891), p. 95

[104]*Milwaukee Sentinel,* 16 June 1865. One of the controversies surrounding the battle of Missionary Ridge is whether or not Union soldiers were ordered to assault the ridge or whether they acted spontaneously. Parsons indicates conclusively that the assault was ordered, but a myth about the men taking strategy into their own hands persists to this day.

behind us swinging his hat, told us to go for the top of the ridge, which we did, under the most terrific of grape, canister, and shrapnel that you can imagine."[105]

The first to acknowledge General Sheridan's orders and start up the ridge was the 24th Wisconsin, followed by a swarm of Union blue.[106] The assault up Missionary Ridge was long and arduous. Forty-four cannons fired upon the Union troops from the rebel position atop the ridge, as well as countless rifles. There were ditches to cross, log barricades to climb, and the Confederates rolled large rocks down the hill to slow the advancing Union troops.[107] These obstacles offered some advantage to Union troops as they used them to shield themselves from the Confederate munitions.[108]

Several times during the ascent of the ridge, the men had to stop under cover of these obstacles and rest as it was an exhausting climb. The color bearer of the 24th Wisconsin became too exhausted to go any further. Adjutant MacArthur saw this and seized the regimental colors from the Sergeant. Then cheering the men to follow

---

[105]Parsons, p. 197

[106]Parsons, p. 200.

[107]Wells, p. 61.

[108]*Milwaukee Sentinel*, 16 June 1865.

him, Arthur led the regiment up the ridge.[109] After almost two hours of fighting, the men reached the top of the ridge, opening up a two-mile gap in Confederate lines.[110] Among the first to reach the top of the ridge was the young Adjutant of the 24th Wisconsin who proudly planted the regimental colors atop Missionary Ridge near General Bragg's former headquarters.[111] The break in his lines forced General Bragg to retreat with his Army southward. Thus, the siege of Chattanooga was lifted.[112]

Adjutant MacArthur's heroic action in leading his regiment up the ridge did not go unrecognized. Major Carl von Baumbach, who was commanding the 24th Wisconsin in this battle due to the absence of Lieutenant Colonel West, recommended his Adjutant to Secretary of War Edwin Stanton for the Medal of Honor. Von Baumbach wrote:

---

[109]Michael Hendrick Fitch, *The Chattanooga Campaign* (Madison: Wisconsin History Commission, 1911), p. 228; and *Milwaukee Sentinel*, 16 June 1865.

[110]*Milwaukee Sentinel*, 16 June 1865; and Fitch, p. 228; and Parsons, p. 197. Manchester, p. 16 says that the charge up Missionary Ridge lasted only forty minutes. This hardly seems probable and accounts of the battle agree that the fighting lasted for nearly two hours.

[111]Watrous, p. 771. There was a dispute about which regiment ascended the ridge first, but it is certain that the 24th was among the first to reach the top of Missionary Ridge (see Parsons, p. 197).

[112]Wells, p. 61.

I beg leave to submit the name of First Lieutenant Arthur MacArthur, Jr., adjutant of the regiment, for consideration under Section 6, Act of March 3, 1863, wherein provision is made for the distribution of medals of honor 'to such persons as most distinguished themselves in action....'

The forcing of Missionary Ridge may be considered as one of the finest assaults in the annals of the war.

The position was a commanding one, the works were strong, the defenders numerous and brave, and the approaches difficult both by nature and art, but the charging line went through or over them to a successful issue on the summit of the ridge.

Among the many acts of personal intrepidity on that memorable occasion none are worthy of higher commendation than that of young MacArthur, then only 18 years old, who, seizing the colors of his regiment at a critical moment, contributed materially to the general result. I remain impressed, now, as I was then, by a sense of the vast importance of this officer's splendid effort on that occasion;

I think it no disparagement to others to declare 'that he was most distinguished in action' on a field where many in the regiment displayed conspicuous gallantry, worthy of the highest praise.

In consideration of the above facts, I recommend that a medal of honor be presented to First Lieutenant Arthur MacArthur, Jr., Adjutant

Twenty-Fourth Wisconsin Infantry Volunteers for 'coolness and conspicuous bravery in seizing the colors of his regiment at a critical moment and planting them on the captured works on the crest of Missionary Ridge, November 25, 1863.[113]

The original recommendation was lost for some time, but MacArthur eventually received the medal of honor for his actions at the battle of Missionary Ridge, twenty-seven years later, on June 30, 1890 when a review of Civil War medals corrected the oversight.[114]

Arthur MacArthur's heroic action was also recognized by his peers. Three days after the battle of Missionary Ridge, Major von Baumbach resigned his commission, and Arthur MacArthur was promoted from Lieutenant to Major to fill the vacancy. Captain E.B. Parsons wrote to Judge MacArthur, "Arthur was magnificent. He seems to be afraid of nothing. He'd fight a pack of tigers in a jungle. He seems the hero of the regiment. As you know, vacancies among the officers are now filled by vote and Arthur, by unanimous agreement, has been elevated to the rank of Major."[115]

---

[113]"Letter of Major Carl von Baumbach to the Secretary of War, 7 June 1890." In MacArthur Correspondence, National Archives.

[114]Lee and Henschel, p. 15.

[115]Carroon, "The Judge and the General," p. 7.

On November 28, 1863, the 24th Wisconsin accompanied the movement of the Fourth Army Corps through London, Tennessee, to relieve the Confederate siege of Knoxville. They arrived there on December 7 and broke the siege. During the next two months, the regiment engaged in various minor movements in the vicinity of Knoxville. In January 1864, the regiment was stationed in London, Tennessee, twenty eight miles from Knoxville where it remained in performance of provost duty until the Spring campaign commenced.[116] Then, on May 3, 1864, the 24th Wisconsin joined General Sherman's Army in Chattanooga as it was about to begin the campaign to Atlanta.[117]

The 24th Wisconsin began the march to Atlanta under the command of Colonel Theodore S. West.[118] Major MacArthur was now second in command. The regiment participated in all thirteen battles of the Atlanta campaign. The campaign to Atlanta was a strategic chess match between General Sherman, one of the North's greatest Generals, and General Joseph E. Johnston, one of the South's ablest commanders. The campaign involved a series of movements with Sherman trying to outflank

---

[116]*Milwaukee Sentinel*, 16 June 1865.

[117]Ibid; and Estabrook, p. 146.

[118]*Roster of Wisconsin Volunteers*, p. 256. Theodore S. West was promoted from Lieutenant Colonel to Colonel on March 4, 1864, creating the vacancy for MacArthur's promotion.

Johnston and Johnston strategically retreating at the last moment to hold Sherman in check and draw him further from his source of supplies.

The initial battle of the campaign took place at Resaca, Georgia on May 14 and 15, 1864.[119] In that battle, Colonel West was seriously wounded and would later resign.[120] This left Major MacArthur in command of the regiment. On June 8, MacArthur received a commission as Lieutenant Colonel from the Governor of Wisconsin.[121] This promotion made MacArthur the youngest Colonel in the Union Army, having just celebrated his nineteenth birthday. Because of this, he earned the nickname the "Boy Colonel," by which he was known and admired throughout the western Army.[122]

MacArthur continued to prove himself worthy of his rank. On June 2, 1864, MacArthur was ordered to lead a reconnaissance mission before Kennesaw Mountain,

---

[119]"MacArthur to Buck, 15 May 1864" in RG 20 MacArthur Archives. 'Buck', who is not identified further in this letter, was Horace Buchanan who had been a Sergeant Major and was elevated to Adjutant and First Lieutenant on May 3, 1864.

[120]*Roster of Wisconsin Volunteers*, p. 256. West never returned to action after he was wounded and he resigned on May 12, 1865.

[121]*Roster of Wisconsin Volunteers*, p. 256; and Carroon, "The Judge and the General", pp. 7-8.

[122]"Arthur MacArthur" in *Outlook*, (September 21, 1912), p. 95; and Usher, p. 1842.

Georgia. Arthur handled the task skillfully, ascertaining the enemy position while conserving manpower. MacArthur's unit reported only two men killed and eleven wounded,[123] a remarkably low number, as reconnaissance missions generally suffered a very high number of casualties.

Undoubtedly, the Republicans feared that if the War Democrats formed a third party it could conceivably split the pro-Union vote enough to allow the Copperheads to win the election. Likewise, the War Democrats were determined to stop the Copperheads and realized Sherman abandoned his war of maneuver and launched an assault upon the Confederate position atop Kennesaw Mountain with a force of 13,500 men.[124] Among the units chosen to make this attack was the 24th Wisconsin, led by Arthur MacArthur. As Union forces stormed the Confederate position, a rebel bullet struck MacArthur's right wrist. He refused to leave the field and continued to lead his regiment in the assault until a second Confederate bullet struck him in the chest. MacArthur was at first thought to be dead, but a packet of letters that he carried in his breast pocket stopped the bullet short of his heart.[125]

---

[123]Usher, p. 1842

[124]Wells, p. 75.

[125]MacArthur, p. 9; and *Milwaukee Sentinel*, 6 September 1912; and *Circulars*.

The attack on Kennesaw Mountain was a disaster for the Union Army, which lost 2,200 men in the attack to only 200 for the Confederates.[126] Despite his injuries, Arthur was out of action for only a week.

MacArthur performed another remarkable reconnaissance mission, this time before Atlanta, on July 19, in which his unit suffered no casualties.[127] The 24th Wisconsin participated in the attack on Jonesboro on August 25, 1864, which cut the last rail line supplying Atlanta.[128] A week later, the new Confederate commander, John B. Hood, who had replaced Johnston in July, was forced to evacuate Atlanta. This victory was a major boost to northern morale and an important factor in Lincoln's re-election two months later.

After evacuating Atlanta, Hood's Army marched northward to Tennessee, attempting to divert Sherman back out of Georgia. Sherman sent a portion of his Army back to Tennessee to deal with Hood, while the bulk of the Union force began its famous march to the sea. Among the troops sent to Tennessee was the 24th Wisconsin, which reached Chattanooga on September 24, 1864.[129]

---

[126]Wells, p. 75.

[127]Usher, p. 1842

[128]Wells, p. 78.

[129]Estabrook, p. 157.

In early October, Arthur left for Milwaukee on furlough to visit his father and younger brother.[130] He returned to his regiment in Tennessee later that same month.[131]

The 24th Wisconsin was in Franklin, Tennessee, on November 30, 1864, when General John B. Hood, with a force of 40,000 Confederates, attacked the Union Army commanded by General John Schofield. Hood's attack was hasty but nearly successful as the center of the Union line began to give way. The 24th Wisconsin was being held in reserve at the time. MacArthur ascertained the situation and, without receiving orders, waved his sword in the air and ordered his men forward to repair the breach in the Union lines. As the "Boy Colonel" led his men forward, they were joined by other regiments. The counterattack saved the day for the Union Army. The Union lines were restored, and the Confederates suffered heavy losses.

MacArthur was seriously wounded in the attack, first in the shoulder, then in the left breast and in the left leg. As he lay wounded in the trenches, MacArthur cheered on

---

[130]Carroon, "The Judge and the General," pp. 7-8.

[131]MacArthur, p. 9, relates an episode where Arthur led his men to vote in the presidential election of 1864, but he was refused because he was too young to vote. In protest, none of the men in the regiment voted, and they chased the election commissioners out of their camp. This is a myth as the 24th voted in the 1864 election.

his men, yelling "Give 'em hell 24th!"[132] as they pursued the retreating rebels. MacArthur spent the next several months recuperating from his wounds in Nashville. Major General David S. Stanley, commanding the 4th Corps, wrote, after the battle of Franklin, "I will not absolutely say that the 24th Wisconsin saved the battle of Franklin, but I can testify from the evidence of my own eyes that they had a great deal to do with it. In this feat of arms, the regiment was gallantly and well-led by young Colonel Arthur MacArthur, who, I hope, may always be a model of goodness and virtue for our young men as he certainly is for bravery and manliness."[133]

After the battle of Franklin, the 24th Wisconsin returned to Nashville with General Schofield where it joined the Army under the command of General Thomas. The regiment participated in the battle of Nashville on December 15 and 16, 1864, which decisively defeated Hood's Army. MacArthur was not well enough to participate in this battle. After the battle of Nashville, the 24th Wisconsin pursued the Confederate Army south into Alabama. It was engaged in various movements in Alabama and Tennessee during the early months of 1865. MacArthur recovered and resumed command of the regiment in early spring. The regiments last action was

---

[132]Wells, p. 78.

[133]Usher, p. 1843.

pursuing guerillas near Allen's Bridge, Tennessee, on April 14, 1865.[134] The 24th Wisconsin returned to Nashville on April 24, 1865,[135] after Lee's surrender at Appomattox. On March 13, 1865, MacArthur was awarded the rank of brevet Colonel for his meritorious service in the Atlanta campaign and the battle of Franklin.[136]

When the 24th Wisconsin left Nashville to return to Milwaukee in June, 1865, the boy Adjutant, who had been laughed at on parade when the regiment left for the front three years earlier, returned as its commander and as Wisconsin's foremost hero of the Civil War. Union Depot in Milwaukee was crowded with thousands of friends, relatives, and former comrades of the men of the "Milwaukee Regiment" when they returned home on Thursday, June 15, 1865. There was a great deal of emotion and disorder as the men of the 24th, now only one-third of the number that had left Milwaukee in 1862, departed the train.

After an initial reunion with friends and relatives, the men fell in line. Colonel MacArthur then led them on parade through the city, escorted by their former comrades and members of the reception committee which had been appointed for the occasion. The parade made its way

---

[134]Carroon, "The Judge and the General," p. 8.

[135]Estabrook, p. 147

[136]*Circulars*

through downtown Milwaukee until it reached the Fair building where a dinner had been prepared for the returning heroes. After the dinner, the men of the regiment adjourned to the main building for speeches. The *Milwaukee Sentinel* reported that four to five thousand people were present for the occasion. Milwaukee Mayor Tallmadge greeted the men and introduced George W. Allen, Esq., who delivered the main address.[137] Next, former Wisconsin Governor Saloman, who had originally given young Arthur his commission as Adjutant of the regiment, welcomed home the men, as did General John Starkweather. Finally, Colonel MacArthur spoke on behalf of the men of the 24th Wisconsin. MacArthur thanked the citizens of Milwaukee for their support and their hospitable reception. Then, he led the regiment in giving three cheers for the citizens of Milwaukee. The regiment then marched to Camp Washburn where it was discharged.[138]

The regiment had been formally mustered out of service on June 10, 1865, while en route from Nashville to Milwaukee. Subsequently, on June 13, Arthur MacArthur was commissioned Colonel of the 24th Wisconsin, but not mustered.[139] The boy Adjutant returned to Milwaukee as a

---

[137]*Milwaukee Sentinel*, 16 June 1865.

[138]Ibid.

[139]*Circulars.*

full Colonel. The "Milwaukee Regiment" was home and the city welcomed its heroes with a great deal of adulation. It must have been a very happy occasion for young Arthur MacArthur, who had only recently celebrated his twentieth birthday.

The War had been everything Arthur could have hoped for in a military career, and he had attained great success. Indeed, to return a conquering hero and commander of the regiment must have given him a great deal of satisfaction. No longer was he the awkward young boy with the squeaky voice who had left Milwaukee amidst laughter and sneers four years earlier. He was now a man who had found his calling and he was determined to remain a soldier.

Even before his unit was mustered out of service, Arthur began to seek support to obtain a commission in the regular Army. One June 5, 1865, Major General David S. Stanley wrote to Secretary of War, Edwin Stanton, telling him that, "Col. MacArthur will fill any position in the regular Army, up to his present rank, with credit."[140] His recommendation was seconded two months later by one of the nation's most distinguished generals, Philip Sheridan, who wrote to the Secretary of War on August 20, 1865:

---

[140]"David S. Stanley to Edwin Stanton, 5 June 1865," in MacArthur Correspondence, National Archives.

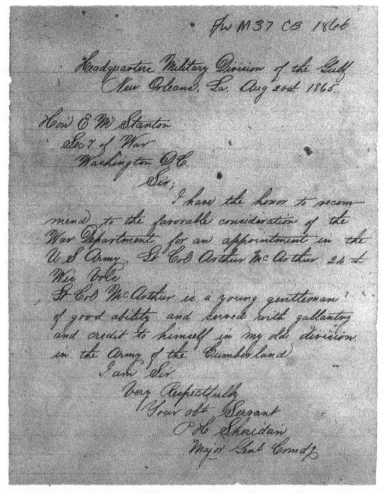

Letter of General Philip Sheridan to Secretary of War Stanton recommending Arthur Jr. for appointment in the regular Army

I have the honor to recommend to the favorable consideration of the War Department for an appointment in the U.S. Army, Lt. Col. Arthur McArthur, 24th Wis. Vols. Lt. Col. MacArthur is a young gentleman of good ability and served with gallantry and credit to himself in my old division in the Army of the Cumberland."[141]

But a career in the severely reduced regular Army was no certainty and must also have made MacArthur sad and uneasy. The War's end forced him to make dramatic readjustments in his life. In the military, Arthur was at home. It had provided him with a sense of belonging and security as had the King's Corner gang during his boyhood. Now all that was gone, and Arthur was left with a sense of uncertainty. He now faced the question of what to do with the rest of his life if his dream of a military career would no longer be possible.

---

[141]"Major General Philip Sheridan to E.M. Stanton, 20 August 1865," in MacArthur Correspondence, National Archives.

Chapter III
The Frontier Days

*"He was, I think, the youngest captain appointed
in the regular army in '66 and one of the best."*

— Charles King[142]

The end of the War marked a difficult period of readjustment for twenty-year-old Arthur MacArthur. He had several ceremonial functions to perform, among them, leading the Fourth of July parade through downtown Milwaukee, alongside General Frederick C. Winkler.[143] The "Boy Colonel" was the toast of the town, but this adoration naturally soon began to fade away. With an appointment to the regular Army still uncertain, young Arthur now had to settle

---

[142]*Charles King Papers*, SHSW.

[143]Carroon, "The Judge and the General," p. 8.

down and decide what to do with the rest of his life if his goal of a career in the military eluded him.

Arthur began this period of readjustment by studying law under his father's tutelage.[144] Judge MacArthur had hoped his son would follow in his footsteps. If Arthur chose to enter the legal profession, Judge MacArthur would have been able to open up many opportunities for him, and Arthur would almost certainly be assured of success. But the martial ardor the War had awakened in young Arthur could not be extinguished.

Although he began studying law, Arthur never gave up on his goal of continuing his military career. Few other professions could provide the structured order that Arthur had grown accustomed to and felt secure in. He could not turn his back on his remarkably successful in his military career and he remained determined to find a way to resume it.[145] The problem was that MacArthur's career choice offered little opportunity for advancement, such as he had experienced during the Civil War, as the United States entered an era of steady cutbacks in the military. A career in the private sector would certainly have offered greater opportunities for success and been more

---

[144]Carol Morris Petillo, *Douglas MacArthur: The Philippine Years* (Ph.D. Dissertation, Rutgers – The State University of New Jersey, 1979) p. 6. This source will hereafter be cited as Petillo, Dissertation; and James, p. 16; and MacArthur, p. 12; and Manchester, p. 20.

[145]*Circulars.*

financially lucrative. These things were not, however, important for young Arthur. He felt comfortable and at home wearing the uniform of a soldier. Arthur was determined to be the best soldier he could be. With that type of determination, all obstacles, no matter how difficult they appear, are surmountable. Though Judge MacArthur had always hoped for Arthur to follow in his footsteps, he fully supported his son's career choice.

Despite the glowing recommendations that Arthur Jr. had received from his former superiors in the military, and Judge MacArthur's extensive political connections, he could only obtain a commission as a Second Lieutenant in the 17th Infantry when he enlisted in the regular Army on February 23, 1866. That same day, he was promoted to First Lieutenant.[146] MacArthur thus began his career in the regular Army with the same rank he held at the beginning of the Civil War.

It was a common occurrence for Officers who had held high ranks during the War to have to accept a lower rank in the post-War Army. This was the inevitable result of the drastic reduction in the size of the Army following the Civil War. Military spending steadily declined after the War and the Army's total strength seldom exceeded twenty-five thousand men.[147] More men had participated

---

[146]*Circulars.*

[147]James, p. 18.

in a relatively insignificant battle in the Civil War than now comprised the entire United States Army.

Still, MacArthur's next promotion came quickly. On July 28, 1866, he was made a Captain in the 36th Infantry, which he joined in New York City.[148] This would be as far as MacArthur's Civil War record would take him in the post-War Army. It would be nearly twenty-three years before Arthur would receive his next promotion. Throughout these years, Judge MacArthur continued to use his extensive political and military contacts to seek promotions and transfers to advance his son's career.[149] Meanwhile, Arthur concentrated on being the best soldier he could be, in hopes that his superiors would recognize his hard work.

Throughout his life, Arthur always relished the opportunity to prove himself in the face of adversity. First, as a junior member of the King's Corner gang, Arthur had to prove that he could hold his own with the older boys, and he was very successful. Then, as the boy Adjutant, ridiculed by his comrades in the 24th Wisconsin regiment, Arthur had to rise to the occasion again to prove he belonged in the regiment. Once more, he was remarkably successful. Now he had to work exceptionally hard and be patient, as opportunities for advancement were few and

---

[148]Ibid.; *Circulars*; and Usher, p. 1845.

[149]Petillo, p. 7.

far between. Arthur was undoubtedly aware of this when he made his decision to join the regular Army, but as always, he was supremely confident he could overcome these obstacles.

In the fall of 1866, the 36th Infantry was assigned to Fort Kearney in the Nebraska Territory. Military life on the western frontier was dramatically different from what Arthur MacArthur had experienced during the Civil War. The main duties of his regiment were to protect travelers along the Oregon trail and the workers building the Union Pacific Railroad. As construction on the Union Pacific Railroad moved westward, the regiment moved along with the workers constructing it to protect them from Indian raids. In 1867, the 36th Infantry was assigned to Fort Sanders in the Wyoming Territory. In May 1868, the regiment was transferred to Fort Bridger in the Wyoming Territory. MacArthur was stationed there when the Union Pacific and Central Pacific Railroads were linked nearby. In 1869, continual budget reductions in military expenditures forced the consolidation of the 7th and 36th Infantries. MacArthur was left temporarily unassigned as he was far down on the list of Captains in seniority. This being the case, he obtained a leave and returned to Milwaukee in the summer of 1869.[150]

---

[150]James, p. 19.

Since the end of the War, Judge MacArthur had remained active in Milwaukee society. He gave up the Presidency of the St. Andrew's Society in 1866, but he continued his involvement with the organization. In 1867, President Andrew Johnson appointed Judge MacArthur as United States Commissioner to the Exposition in Paris, France.[151] This appointment indicates the extent to which Judge MacArthur's influence had expanded outside of his own state. In 1868, Judge MacArthur opened up a law office in Chicago with A.D. Rich and H.H. Thomas, while continuing to serve as Judge of the 2nd District Circuit Court in Milwaukee. That same year Arthur MacArthur Sr. married Zolia C. Hodges, the daughter of Nehemiah Hodges of North Adams, Massachusetts. The wedding was held in Chicago on January 29, 1868.[152] Judge MacArthur and his second wife continued to live in Milwaukee at the MacArthur home on Van Buren Street. When Arthur Jr. returned home in the summer of 1869 to visit his father and brother Frank, who was now fifteen, he also met the Judge's new bride, Zolia.

Arthur spent his free time at the outposts on the western frontier studying. There was very little else for a soldier to do to pass the time, except to drink and gamble, neither of which interested Arthur. MacArthur was

---

[151]Mann, p. 171: and James, p. 9.

[152]*MacArthur Collection*, Milwaukee County Historical Society; and Cartoon, "The Judge and the General," p. 9.

determined to succeed in the military and he realized that he would have to compensate for his lack of formal education if he was to do so. During this time, Arthur had continued to study law. While in Milwaukee in 1869, he was admitted to the practice of law in Wisconsin before the Supreme Court and Federal Courts in the state.[153] This accomplishment must have been especially pleasing to Judge MacArthur who had hoped Arthur would choose a legal career. Arthur's interest in the law was not, however, merely an attempt to please his father. He realized that a sound legal background would be beneficial to his career as an Army officer.

In the fall of 1869, tragedy struck the MacArthur family as Judge MacArthur's second wife, Zolia, died after a brief illness on October 12. The death of his second wife must have been a great loss to Judge MacArthur. Whether or not he had planned to do so prior to his wife's death, Judge MacArthur resigned from the Circuit Court on November 9. The following month, Judge MacArthur moved to Chicago to devote his full attention to his law practice there.[154] Perhaps the elder MacArthur wanted a change of environment after the loss of his second wife.

---

[153]Petillo, Dissertation, p. 103. See note 35.

[154]MacArthur Collection, MCHS. MacArthur sold his home on Van Buren Street on May 11, 1870.

The following year, in July, President Grant appointed Judge MacArthur as an Associate Justice of the Supreme Court of the District of Columbia. In securing this appointment, Judge MacArthur's political contacts paid off for himself. His chief sponsor for this position was Wisconsin Senator Matthew Hale Carpenter, a long-time friend and associate. Carpenter had initially tried to get MacArthur an appointment as Federal Judge for the Western District of Wisconsin, but he was unsuccessful in this attempt as politicians from that part of the state had their own candidate for the post, James C. Hopkins.[155] MacArthur was confirmed as Associate Justice of the Supreme Court of the District of Columbia by the Senate on July 15, 1870, and he took up residence in the nation's capital. Judge MacArthur returned to Wisconsin the following year and married Mary E. Hopkins, the widow of Benjamin Hopkins, a two-term Congressman from the Madison district, on January 14, 1871, at Mrs. Hopkins residence in Madison.[156] Judge MacArthur then returned to Washington, D.C., together with his new bride.

Following his leave in Milwaukee in 1869, Arthur MacArthur Jr. was stationed in New York City as a recruiting officer while awaiting reassignment. While stationed there, MacArthur appealed to General Sheridan,

---

[155]Carroon, "The Judge and the General," p. 9.

[156]*MacArthur Collection*, MCHS; and Mann, p. 171.

asking for a transfer to the Cavalry. His request was denied. Instead, Arthur was assigned to the 13th Infantry, then stationed at Fort Rawlins in the Utah Territory, in the summer of 1870.[157] Arthur had hoped for a transfer to the Cavalry because it would have provided him with better opportunities for advancement and recognition. During this time, the Army was engaged in thirty or more battles each year with Indian tribes on the western frontier,[158] but these engagements largely involved the cavalry. The role of the Infantry on the vast expanse of the western plains was primarily a passive one.

When MacArthur joined the 13th Infantry at Fort Rawlins, he was put in command of Company K of the regiment.[159] Fort Rawlins was a desolate place. The camp had no permanent facilities and the men lived in tents making life very difficult during the harsh winter months.[160] The following year, the regiment was assigned to Camp Stambaugh to protect miners. Conditions in this camp were much the same as at Fort Rawlins. During his time on the desolate frontier, Arthur never stopped looking for intellectual challenges and opportunities to advance his career. In 1872, he sought an appointment as

---

[157]James, pp. 19-20.

[158]Manchester, p. 22.

[159]Petillo, Dissertation, p. 8.

[160]James, p. 20.

an instructor in the Military Department of the University of Wisconsin. Although the President of the University and the Board of Regents backed his request, the Secretary of War refused to give his consent.[161] In the fall of 1873, MacArthur was transferred to Fort Fred Steele in the Wyoming Territory where his company was stationed throughout the following year.[162]

MacArthur's commander in the 13th Infantry was a colorful Frenchman, Colonel Philippe Regis de Trobriand, whose father had served under Napoleon. His family's previous political connections limited his opportunities in France, so the young man emigrated to the United States in 1841. He married an American woman, Mary Mason Jones, the daughter of a wealthy banker.

Philippe Regis de Trobriand

---

[161]"Letter to the President of the University of Wisconsin, 17 June 1872." In MacArthur Correspondence, National Archives.

[162]Ibid.

During the Civil War, he had served as a Union General, distinguishing himself at the battle of Gettysburg. Trobriand was a highly educated man who had been a novelist, artist, and journalist in both France and the United States. During his service in the west, Trobriand wrote a journal that was later published as *Army Life in Dakota*. It was widely acclaimed for its portrayal of Army life on the western frontier.[163] Indeed, Trobriand must have been an impressive man to serve under, especially for someone like Arthur MacArthur, who had developed strong and diverse scholarly interests.

The routine duties of the regiment were quite dull and left the men with a great deal of free time. Many men spent this time drinking, gambling, and socializing. These leisure time activities held very little interest for Arthur MacArthur, driven by his goal of success in his military career. Perhaps, his achievements during the Civil War left him feeling that he was destined to greatness. MacArthur spent his free time engaged in studies.[164] Arthur's broad

---

[163]Philippe Regis de Trobriand, *Army Life in Dakota* (Chicago: Lakeview Press, 1941). James, pp. 20-21. James suggest Trobriand may have been a model after whom Arthur patterned himself. I think this unlikely. Rather, MacArthur's broad scholarly interests grew out of his desire for success and he would likely have followed this same path had he never known Trobriand.

[164]Fant, p. 14. Fant suggests that Arthur spent a great deal of time leading his men against raiding Indians. This is not true. MacArthur saw little combat on the frontier.

range of scholarly interests included law, political science, and history. MacArthur viewed each of these disciplines as essential knowledge for an Army Officer. His favorite study was history,[165] which was perhaps the most relevant subject for a soldier.

The wide range of MacArthur's studies also suggests that he viewed the Army's role in American society broadly, to include civil as well as military functions. MacArthur's friend and fellow soldier, Charles King, later recalled that Arthur, "set himself vigorously to preparation for the duties of the future. He who had seen little of school and nothing of college became speedily known as the student of the service."[166] The impetus for MacArthur's scholarly pursuits had always been the achievement of his clear goal that he had defined as success in a military career. Life on the frontier was difficult, and MacArthur expressed no particular romantic fondness for it. Still, he was careful to take advantage of the opportunities it offered him to prepare himself for the future.

In October of 1874, the 13th Infantry was transferred to Jackson Barracks, Louisiana, where its primary duty was to bolster the Radical Republican regime of Governor

---

[165]*Milwaukee Journal*, 6 September 1912.

[166]*Charles King Papers*, SHSW.

William P. Kellogg.[167] The task was an unpleasant one as there was a great deal of opposition to Kellogg's administration. Still, Louisiana must have been a very comfortable place to be stationed for men who had spent several years on the western frontier. While in New Orleans during the winter of 1874, MacArthur met twenty-two-year-old Mary Pinkney Hardy, the daughter of a cotton merchant from Norfolk, Virginia.[168]

Mary Pinkney Hardy was born on May 22, 1852, at the family home near Norfolk, known as Riverredge. Her father, Thomas Hardy, was a successful cotton merchant. Pinky, as she was called, was one of fourteen children. The Hardy family spent summers at their farm in Henderson, North Carolina, known as Burnside.[169] With the outbreak of the Civil War, the Hardy's left Norfolk for the relative security of North Carolina. Six of Pinky's brothers served under General Robert E. Lee with the Confederate Army in Virginia.[170] During the War, the Hardy family home in Norfolk was used as a Union hospital and later served as the Headquarters for Major General Benjamin Butler. When the War was over, the Hardys moved to Baltimore, Maryland for a couple of years. While in Baltimore,

---

[167]James, p. 21.

[168]MacArthur, p. 8.

[169]Petillo, p. s.

[170]James, p. 23; and Petillo, Dissertation, p. 11.

Pinky[171] attended Mount de Sales Academy. The family later returned to Riverredge.

Pinky was very fond of travel. A very ambitious young lady, she often accompanied her father on business trips. [172] On one such trip to New Orleans in 1874, she met twenty-nine-year-old Captain Arthur MacArthur. Their son Douglas later related that their meeting was "love at first sight."[173] Certainly, the short duration of their courtship attests to this. The young couple corresponded throughout the next Spring. In May 1875, Arthur obtained a three-month leave of absence and journeyed to Riverredge to claim his bride. Arthur and Pinky were married at the Hardy family home on May 19, 1875.[174] Several of Pinky's brothers refused to attend the wedding because their sister was marrying a Yankee officer.[175] The bitterness between the North and South had not yet healed. In Arthur, Pinky found someone who was as ambitious as herself and who offered her the opportunity for travel and adventure that she cherished.[176] Arthur's ambition dictated that he would only marry a woman who

---

[171]MacArthur, p. 14.

[172]Petillo, Dissertation, p. 12-13.

[173]MacArthur, p. 14.

[174]Petillo, Dissertation, p. 13.

[175]James, p. 23.

[176]Petillo, Dissertation, pp. 12-13.

could understand his dedication in pursuit of the goals he had set for himself.

After his leave of absence, MacArthur was temporarily assigned to serve on the Examining and Retiring Board in Washington, D.C., where he served for one year.[177] While in Washington, he introduced his bride to Judge MacArthur and his third wife. Arthur's younger brother Frank was now studying at Harvard University and planned to follow in his father's footsteps and enter the legal profession.[178] Judge MacArthur was undoubtedly pleased that one of his sons had chosen to enter the legal profession, and he spared no expense to ensure that Frank received the finest education. After graduating from Harvard in 1876, Frank studied law in New York City until 1880, when he was admitted to the New York Bar Association. After his admission to the Bar, Frank worked in the United States Patent Office in New York City.[179]

Judge MacArthur was always eager to help his sons advance in their careers in any way possible. Since his move to Washington, D.C., in 1870, Arthur Sr. had made many new contacts and became a very active member of the local community. The Judge had always had a fondness for social activities, and he quickly became a

---

[177]James, p. 23.

[178]Mann, p. 172; and MacArthur, p. 5.

[179]Mann, p. 172.

popular guest at social gatherings in the nation's capital.[180] His outgoing personality, combined with intelligence, wit, and geniality, had always made Judge MacArthur a popular man.

While living in Washington D.C., Judge MacArthur served as President of the Washington Humane Society, President of the Associated Charities of the District of Columbia, and President of the Board of Regents of the National University.[181] These activities reflect his prominent social position in Washington, D.C. It was reported that "Judge MacArthur has always been prominent in what is known as the official society of Washington. Of a genial nature, fond of dining out and always ready with a fund of stories to amuse, he was a frequent and popular guest at many social gatherings."[182] Judge MacArthur's third wife, Mary, must also have been a great help to him. As her former husband was a Congressman, she was undoubtedly familiar with Washington social life. In addition, he had rapidly developed a reputation as a distinguished jurist. Judge MacArthur and his wife opened up many opportunities for Arthur and Pinky during the year they spent in Washington, D.C.

---

[180]*The Evening Wisconsin*, 27 August 1896.

[181]MacArthur, p. 5; and Mann, p. 171.

[182]*Evening Wisconsin*, 27 August 1896.

On August 1, 1876, the first of three sons was born to Arthur and Pinky MacArthur. In accordance with family tradition, the child was named Arthur. Pinky had returned to Norfolk for the birth of her son in order to be with her mother. In the Fall of 1876, Arthur was sent back to Louisiana and resumed command of Company K of the 13th Infantry.[183] During the next several years, the MacArthurs spent time at various posts in Louisiana and Arkansas.

In mid-1877, Captain MacArthur and the 13th Infantry was sent to Pennsylvania to deal with labor unrest in the mining areas of Scranton and Wilkesbarre. The regiment performed its task effectively and restored order without any bloodshed.[184] The following year Pinky was again pregnant and returned home to her family with her young son Arthur. The MacArthurs second son, Malcom, was born on October 17, 1878 at New Britain, Connecticut where the Hardy family was vacationing.[185] Pinky returned to Louisiana with her two sons later that year.

Life in the posts of Louisiana and Arkansas was very different from the year the young couple had spent in Washington, D.C. Arthur continued to spend his free time pursuing his studies, while Pinky raised their two sons. In

---

[183]James, p. 24.

[184]Ibid.; and Petillo, Dissertation, p. 14.

[185]James, p. 23.

Arthur, Jr. with his wife Pinky
and sons Arthur III and Douglas

January 1880, Pinky was pregnant again and prepared to return to Riverredge for the birth of her third child. Pinky went into labor before she left for Virginia and the MacArthurs' third son was born prematurely at Arsenal Barracks in Little Rock, Arkansas on January 26, 1880.[186] The couple named their third son Douglas, and he would achieve great fame following in the footsteps of his father.

In July 1880, MacArthur and his Company were again transferred to the western frontier. This time he was assigned to Fort Wingate in the New Mexico Territory. The routine and dullness of frontier life was something that

---

[186]MacArthur, p. 14.

Arthur had learned to deal with over the years by applying himself to his studies. For Pinky, this was a new and not altogether pleasant experience. She was an active and outgoing person, and the frontier provided few opportunities for her. She contented herself with raising her three sons. Throughout these years, the 13th Infantry had an average strength of 440 men. The single biggest problem facing regimental commanders was maintaining the strength of their units. Between 1881 and 1882, the regiment suffered 248 desertions, and replacements were slow in arriving.[187] MacArthur tried to keep his Company as efficient as possible despite the challenging conditions faced by the men.

Arthur, Jr. did not possess the outgoing personality of his father. His relationship with the troops under his command was friendly but formal. He seldom participated in the social events and informal gatherings that characterized Army life on the frontier.[188] Socializing held little interest for Arthur, who was austere, serious-minded, and a strict disciplinarian. These personality traits undoubtedly developed over the years as he worked hard to overcome the difficulties he faced in pursuit of his goals with great seriousness of purpose. He had developed these traits early in life to compensate for his youth, and,

---

[187]James, p. 25.

[188]Ibid.; and Petillo, p. 14.

Fort Wingate, New Mexico

although age was no longer a factor as the years passed, these traits remained and characterized his personality throughout the remainder of his life.

During this his time on the frontier, Arthur devoted himself to his studies, not only warfare but of the strategic position of the United States in the world. He began to take a great interest in affairs in the Pacific and he began to develop some very definite ideas about the importance of that region to the strategic interests of the country.

He continued to seek advancement and to escape the monotony of life on the frontier. MacArthur took the initiative to request an appointment as military attaché to China, and he sought to enlist the support of former President Grant to obtain the appointment. Grant, a

longtime friend of Judge MacArthur, whom he had
appointed to the Supreme Court of the District of
Columbia, write to Arthur, Sr. from New York on June 10,
1882:

> Since my conversation with the Captain a few weeks
> since, seeing the interest he has taken in Eastern
> affairs, and the study he has given the subject, I am
> not only satisfied that his selection would be the
> wisest that could be made, but that the appointment
> of such an attaché to our Chinese Legation might be
> attended with good results in establishing better
> relations with those people.

Grant did, however, suspect that obtaining the
appointment would be difficult in the political
environment of that time. The former President continued:

> I know there is a sort of morbid sensitiveness on the
> part of Congress and the press generally against
> trusting soldiers anywhere except in front of the
> cannon or musket. But if the matter is laid before the
> President I will willingly give my views in favor of
> such an appointment, and of the selection of Capt.
> MacArthur for the place.[189]

---

[189]"Ulysses S. Grant to Arthur MacArthur, 10 June 1882," in
Records of the War Department, National Archives, Record Group
165.

To support his case, Arthur Jr. prepared a forty-four-page report entitled "Chinese Memorandum and Notes." In this report, he demonstrated an awareness of the growing importance of the far East, and he considered the involvement of the United States in the region to be essential. He argued:

> It is not too much to assert that the American Republic can never acquire its full complement of riches and power, if it permits itself to be excluded from the field of Asiatic commerce; or even if it allows restrictions to be placed upon its communications with that continent... we cannot attain our natural growth, or even continue to exist as a commanding and progressive nationality, unless we secure and maintain the sovereignty of the Pacific.[190]

He feared the weakness of the Chinese Empire would subject it to the domination of Russia. He warned:

> A Collision... between Russia and China alone would be a matter of vast importance. It could not be confined to Central Asia. It would resound on the

---

[190]"Chinese Memorandum and Notes," pp. 9-10 in Records of the War Department, National Archives, Record Group 165.

shores of the Pacific, and affect the commerce of the world.[191]

MacArthur argued that "in the civilized parts of the world, there are now only two typical governmental ideas: The Imperial and the Republican — the American and the Russian."[192] there was a need for competent military officers to observe the military development of the Chinese.

He also demonstrated a good understanding of economics and argued that "the extension of our commerce is absolutely essential to the prosperity and happiness of our citizens."[193] MacArthur observed the impact of the Industrial Revolution on the American economy, and he surmised, "We must have new and ever-expanding markets to meet our ever-increasing powers of production; and these seem to lie principally in the far East, and there, we naturally and inevitably must go."[194]

He viewed the Russian Empire as the greatest threat to American interests in the Pacific basin, arguing that "Russia once settled in supremacy, there can be no doubt that restrictions would be introduced by which the natural

---

[191]"Chinese Memorandum and Notes," p. 8 in Records of the War Department, National Archives, Record Group 165.

[192]Ibid., p. 11.

[193]Ibid., p. 18.

[194]Ibid., p. 44.

development of trade would be troubled, monopolies fostered, and all possibility of a free and truly cosmopolitan intercourse with Asia effectually destroyed."[195] MacArthur argued that the United States needed to pay more attention to developing defenses for the Pacific coast, stating "it seems inevitable that the Empire and the Republic are destined to meet in Asia."[196]

He concluded his Memorandum, arguing for the assignment of a military officer to the U.S. Legation in Peking:

> from a purely military standpoint China affords an immense field for practical observation. A competent army officer would undoubtedly find abundant and exceedingly profitable employment near the Chinese Mission of the United States.[197]

As Grant had predicted, MacArthur's request for transfer to China was denied, and he returned to Fort Wingate. Arthur certainly felt dejected. It had been sixteen years since his last promotion, and he had experienced little advancement during that time. Certainly, he felt that

---

[195]Ibid., p. 19.

[196]"Chinese Memorandum and Notes," p. 13 in Records of the War Department, National Archives, Record Group 165. MacArthur stated that "Russia has no interest in Asia except her own aggrandizement., p. 32.

[197]Ibid., p. 28.

his skills were being wasted in the far west. Nevertheless, he did not let his disappointment make him lose sight of his goals. He continued to await the day when his abilities would be recognized.

In April 1883, MacArthur obtained a leave of absence, and the family once again traveled to the Hardy home in Norfolk. During their stay at Riverredge, all three of the MacArthur children came down with the measles. On April 12, 1883, tragedy struck the family when four-year-old Malcom died. The child was buried in the Hardy family plot in Norfolk. The loss of their young son must have been a severe blow to the MacArthurs. After this tragedy, they certainly did not cherish the thought of having to journey back to the loneliness of the frontier.

In February 1884, Company K of the 13th Infantry, under the command of Captain MacArthur, was transferred to Fort Selden in the New Mexico Territory, near the border with Mexico. In 1885, Geronimo led his Apaches from their Arizona reservation and began what was to be the last of the Apache Wars. It was mainly the Cavalry that participated in the battles with the Indians. The Apaches also spent a great deal of time raiding into Mexico, which did not involve any American troops. The role of the infantry was mainly to guard the forts to which they were assigned. No major battles took place near Fort Selden, where MacArthur and Company K were stationed, but campaign badges were awarded to those engaged in defensive as well as offensive operations. As a result, MacArthur earned his first campaign badge since the Civil War.

The Apache Wars ended when Geronimo finally surrendered in August, 1886. Despite the fact that MacArthur's Company saw no action in these engagements, he was commended for maintaining his post in excellent military order and for keeping his troops combat ready. The Departmental Inspector, Major G.H. Burton, reported, "The military bearing and appearance of the troops were very fine... Captain MacArthur impresses me as an officer of more than ordinary ability, and very zealous in the performance of duty. The company and post show evidence of intelligent, judicious, and masterly supervision."[198] MacArthur's dedication and hard work were finally being recognized.

During the Fall of 1886, the 13th Infantry was dispersed to various posts. Their presence in the southwest was no longer required due to the end of the Indian Wars. Major General Alexander McCook, commandant of the Infantry and Cavalry School at Fort Leveanworth, Kansas, read the report filed by the Departmental Inspector and remembered the youthful Adjutant who had distinguished himself for his bravery while serving under

---

[198]"Major G.H. Burton to Assistant Adjutant General, Fort Leavenworth, Kansas, 15 September 1885," in MacArthur Correspondence, National Archives.

McCook's command at the battle of Murfreesboro. McCook saw to it that MacArthur and Company K were assigned to Fort Leveanworth.[199]

MacArthur performed his new duties as an administrator and an instructor admirably and continued to impress General McCook. Certainly, Arthur felt that his talents were finally being put to good use. In this new capacity, the time he had spent devoted to his studies while serving on frontier outposts proved to be a great asset. In 1889, a position for a Major in the Adjutant General's Office in Washington, D.C. became available and provided MacArthur with the opportunity to receive his long-awaited promotion.

Judge MacArthur used his extensive political connections to have letters of recommendation written for his son. General McCook, impressed with MacArthur's abilities, supported his application for the position in Washington D.C. McCook wrote to Brigadier General J.C. Kelton, the Adjutant General of the Army:

> I have known Captain MacArthur since 1862, when he joined my command in the Army of the Cumberland with the 24th Wisconsin. He was adjutant of the regiment at the age of seventeen years.

---

[199]James, p. 27.

Captain MacArthur grew to manhood in war; for his ability and marked bravery, he was promoted lieutenant colonel of his regiment, commanding the same in nine battles before reaching his twenty-first year. When opportunity offered, he never failed to distinguish himself, and he has been faithful to every trust since. He is beyond question the most distinguished Captain in the Army of the United States for gallantry and good conduct in war. He is a student, a master of his profession, has legal ability which fits him for the position, is exceptional in habit, temperate at all times, yet modest withal.[200]

On July 1, 1889, MacArthur was promoted to Major and ordered to report to Washington, D.C., where he would serve as an Assistant Adjutant General.[201] That same summer, on June 8, 1889, Arthur was awarded a Doctor of Law degree from the National University, of which Judge MacArthur was President of the Board of Regents. The Law School was the only part of the National University that ever came into operation as the idea to establish the school was later abandoned.[202] Certainly, with the vast amount of study Arthur had done over the years, he was deserving of the degree, and the fact the

---

[200]"McCook to Adjutant General, July 16, 1888," in MacArthur Correspondence, National Archives.

[201]James, p. 28; and Petillo, Dissertation, p. 29.

[202]James, p. 29; and Lee and Henschel, p. 16.

Judge MacArthur was on the Board of Regents should not detract from Arthur's accomplishment. Arthur likely sought the degree to increase his chances of advancement in the Adjutant General's Office, where legal knowledge certainly would be an asset. Judge MacArthur certainly encouraged his son to obtain the degree.

When Arthur and his family moved to Washington, D.C., in 1889, Judge MacArthur no longer served on the Supreme Court of the District of Columbia. Judge MacArthur had retired from the bench a year earlier and "devoted himself to writing and enjoyment of books, of which he possessed a great variety and abundance."[203] In 1886, prior to his retirement from the Court, Judge MacArthur published *Education and its Relation to Manual Industry*, which was a widely acclaimed book. The Judge was especially fond of Shakespeare and made "an elaborate argument refuting the claims of the Bacon adherents. He disposed of the question [of Shakespeare's identity] much as he would if it were an issue before his court, and overruled an appeal."[204] His most acclaimed work was *The Biography of the English Language, with notices of Authors, Ancient and Modern*. Among Judge MacArthur's other literary works were *The Historical Study of Mary Stuart, Essays and Papers on Miscellaneous Topics, Law as*

---

[203]*Evening Wisconsin*, 27 August 1896.

[204]Ibid.

Applied in a Business Education, and his final book, *A History of Lady Jane Grey.*[205]

Following his retirement from the Court, Judge MacArthur had some health problems, and his wife gradually lost her sight.[206] The couple spent their winters in Florida and also lived in New Jersey. Arthur's younger brother Frank, who had been working as an Attorney in the U.S. Patent Office in New York City, married Rose Winston of Tuscumbia, Alabama, on May 19, 1886. That same year, Frank left the Patent Office for the more lucrative opportunities available in private practice. He opened a successful law office in New York City. Frank and Rose MacArthur had one son, born on March 22, 1888, whom they named Malcom. The following year, on December 1, 1889, Frank died suddenly and unexpectedly.[207]

With the exception of the loss of his brother, Arthur's time in Washington D.C. was quite pleasant. In a review of Civil War medals, Arthur finally received the Congressional Medal of Honor for leading his regiment in

---

[205]Ibid.

[206]"Arthur MacArthur to Admiral Walker, 24 January 1891," in RG-20, MacArthur Archives.

[207]Mann, p. 172. Frank was the first to break the family tradition of naming the firstborn son Arthur. Perhaps, they chose the name Malcom in honor of Arthur's son, Malcom, who had died five years earlier.

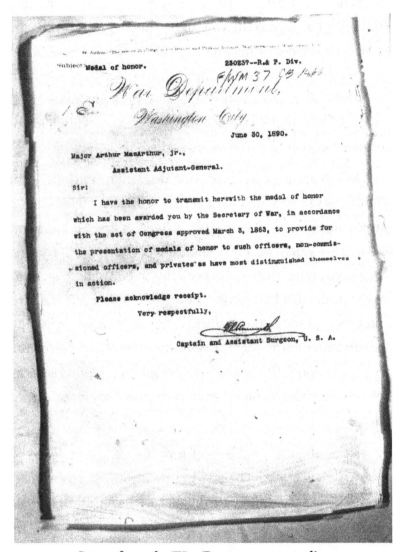

Subject: **Medal of honor.**   230237--R.& P. Div.

War Department,

Washington City

June 30, 1890.

Major Arthur MacArthur, Jr.,

Assistant Adjutant-General.

Sir:

I have the honor to transmit herewith the medal of honor
which has been awarded you by the Secretary of War, in accordance
with the act of Congress approved March 3, 1863, to provide for
the presentation of medals of honor to such officers, non-commis-
sioned officers, and privates as have most distinguished themselves
in action.

Please acknowledge receipt.

Very respectfully,

Captain and Assistant Surgeon, U. S. A.

Letter from the War Department awarding
Arthur MacArthur, Jr. his Medal of Honor

the charge up Missionary Ridge. The medal was awarded on June 30, 1890, nearly twenty-seven years after the battle.[208] The oversight was likely uncovered during the extensive review of his military service record conducted in connection with his application to the Adjutant General's office. In any event, MacArthur finally received the medal he had so bravely earned on the battlefields of Tennessee twenty-seven years earlier.

MacArthur performed his duties in the Adjutant General's Office with characteristic efficiency. He was the junior member of the staff of sixteen Assistant Adjutant Generals. Much of the Office's work involved routine administrative duties, especially record-keeping, but MacArthur also had to opportunity to help draft military reforms. Among the reforms he sponsored was the establishment of merit examinations for officers below the rank of Colonel.[209] He also sponsored innovations such as introducing the canteen and recreation room to Army posts.[210]

Undoubtedly, these reform ideas grew out of MacArthur's experience serving on the western frontier. He had been frustrated by the lack of recognition he had received while serving on isolated frontier posts. Merit

---

[208]Lee and Henschel, p. 15.

[209]James, pp. 29-30.

[210]Usher, p. 1848; and Lee and Henschel p. 16.

examinations certainly seemed to him a better way to evaluate officer's capabilities and allow for fairer promotions. MacArthur viewed the canteen and recreation room as a means to improve morale by helping to alleviate the boredom faced by soldiers on the western frontier and thereby lower desertion rates. This reform was subsequently abolished for financial considerations. MacArthur adamantly, but unsuccessfully, opposed the abolition of the canteen saying, "The amiable people who are behind the anti-canteen movement did not realize what they were doing. I am sure of that or they would never have taken the stand they did."[211]

Arthur's service in the Adjutant General's Office won him high praise from General Kelton. After he had completed his assignment in Washington, D.C., Kelton wrote to him, "I wish to tell you that I regard your assignment to duty in The Adjutant General's Office at the time you were, a most fortunate circumstance for the office and the Army. Every duty assigned to you, you have performed thoroughly and conscientiously. Every recommendation you have made has been consistent and without color of prejudice or favor, but solely for the good of the Army." The General went on to praise MacArthur's work on the reform to require merit examinations for officers below the rank of Colonel, saying, "It places you at

---

[211]*Milwaukee Sentinel*, 6 September 1912.

the head of the military reformers of the Department, where I look for you always to be found."[212]

While Arthur was stationed in Washington D.C., his eldest son, Arthur III, received an appointment to the United States Naval Academy in 1892 from the Oshkosh District of Wisconsin.[213] Arthur MacArthur, Jr. had always maintained Wisconsin to be his home and in fact was a member of the Loyal Legion, a Wisconsin veteran's group. This allowed Arthur III to receive the appointment from Wisconsin. In receiving his appointment, Arthur III benefitted from the contacts that both his father and grandfather had established.

In the Fall of 1893, Arthur was reassigned to Fort Sam Houston, Texas, the Headquarters of the Department of Texas, while he continued to serve as Assistant Adjutant General. The position of Assistant Adjutant General made MacArthur more visible to his superiors. No longer was he isolated in command of a small company in a far off frontier fort. While stationed in San Antonio, the MacArthurs' youngest son, Douglas, began his military training by attending the West Texas Military Academy.

The year 1896 would be eventful for the MacArthur family. In the summer of that year, Arthur III graduated from the Naval Academy and Douglas graduated from the

---

[212]quoted in James, p. 29.

[213]MacArthur, p. 17.

Judge Arthur MacArthur, Sr.

West Texas Military Academy. On August 26, while on a
trip to Atlantic City, Judge MacArthur passed away.[214]
This must have been a particularly dramatic loss for
Arthur. His father had always been there to lend him
support and encouragement. Arthur Sr.'s guidance had

---

[214]*The Evening Wisconsin*, 27 August 1896.

helped Arthur become a successful soldier. 1896 was thus a year of mixed emotions for Arthur. The graduation of his two sons from their respective military academies and the death of his father must have made him feel all of his fifty-one years. To have his two sons graduating and following in his footsteps must also have been rewarding for him.

Arthur continued to impress his superior officers with his skill and efficiency and, on May 26, 1896, he was promoted to the rank of Lieutenant Colonel.[215] The Army was undergoing rapid changes at this time also, and promotions for dedicated, hard-working officers like Arthur MacArthur became more frequent. The United States entered a new paradigm in its foreign policy as it emerged as a world power.[216] Arthur MacArthur, who had persevered through the most difficult times in the Army's history, was now prepared to take a leading role as it entered this new era.

---

[215]MacArthur, p. 17; and *Circulars.*

[216]For a discussion of the new paradigm in American foreign policy, see Robert L. Beisner, *From the Old Diplomacy to the New, 1865-1900* (Arlington Heights, IL: Harlan Davidson Inc., 1975). For an analysis of the changes in the military as the United States entered this new era, see William Addleman Ganoe, *The History of the United States Army* (Ashton, Maryland: Eric Lundberg, 1964).

Chapter IV
The Philippine Experience

"We are planting the best traditions, the best characteristics of Americanism in such a way that they can never be removed from that soil. That in itself seems to me a most inspiring thought."

Arthur MacArthur Jr.[217]

I n October 1897, Lieutenant Colonel MacArthur was transferred to the Department of the Dakotas, with its headquarters in St. Paul, Minnesota,[218] where he continued to serve as Assistant Adjutant General. When Arthur left Fort Sam Houston, Pinky and Douglas did not

---

[217]*Affairs in the Philippine Islands. Hearings before the Committee on the Philippines of the United States Senate.* 57th Congress, 1st Session, Document No. 331, Part 2. (Washington, U.S. Government Printing Office, 1902), p. 869. Hereafter this source will be cited as Senate Documents, No. 331.

[218]James, p. 30; and Petillo, Dissertation. p. 38.

accompany him to his new post. Instead, they moved to Milwaukee, where they lived at the Plankinton House in order for Douglas to prepare for the West Point Examination to be administered in Congressman Theobald Otjen's District. Arthur was often able to return to Milwaukee by train to be with his family on weekends.[219] Arthur certainly enjoyed these opportunities to return to Milwaukee as he always considered it as his home.

While in Milwaukee, Arthur was able to reconnect with many of his boyhood friends and his old comrades from the 24th Wisconsin regiment. Although Douglas had the highest score on the West Point Examination, there was some controversy about Otjen appointing the boy to the military academy. Some people felt that the MacArthurs should no longer be considered residents of Milwaukee, and they charged that Pinky and Douglas came back to the city solely for purposes of the examination. Arthur rallied his Milwaukee friends, as well as friends of the late Judge MacArthur, to write letters to Congressman Otjen on behalf of Douglas. The Milwaukee newspapers also supported the claim that the MacArthurs were residents of Milwaukee, pointing out that Arthur was living in city when he enlisted in the regular Army. They argued that his service in the military in no way affected his residency. A.P. Houston, Secretary of the Commandery of Wisconsin

---

[219]MacArthur, p. 17.

Arthur MacArthur, Jr.

of the Loyal Legion, wrote to Otjen, asserting that Arthur MacArthur, Jr. was a resident of Wisconsin because he could not be a member of the Commandery of the State if he were not.[220] The short-lived controversy soon passed. Douglas received the appointment and entered West Point in June 1899.[221]

After many years of dispute between the United States and Spain over Cuba, conflict erupted when the United States declared war on Spain on April 25, 1898. The Spanish-American War was different from any previous conflict that the United States had been involved in because the War expanded outside of the western hemisphere. This escalation had been by design. Spain had met virtually all of the American demands concerning Cuba, but this still did not satisfy the budding American imperialist ambitions.[222] The Philippine Islands, a remote area that few Americans even knew existed prior to the conflict with Spain, became one of the main areas of conflict.

The Philippine Islands had been a Spanish colony since the sixteenth century. Spain had never made a serious attempt to develop its colony. Wealth was

---

[220]"A.P. Houston to Theobald Otjen, June 13, 1898," in MacArthur Collection, MCHS. There are several other letters in this collection regarding the controversy over Douglas' appointment to West Point.

[221]MacArthur, p. 25.

[222]William J. Pomeroy, *American Neo-Colonialism: Its Emergence in the Philippines and Asia* (New York: International Publishers Co., Inc., 1970), p. 32.

extracted from the Islands to benefit the Spanish government and the Catholic Church, but only a select group of Filipinos realized any benefits from Spanish rule. Spanish domination had been harsh on most Filipinos, and, as a result, Philippine nationalism emerged in the latter part of the nineteenth century. The Philippine Islands was the first of the southeast Asian colonies to experience the development of modern nationalism.[223]

In the early 1890s, the intellectual leader of the Filipino nationalist movement was Jose Rizal. Rizal was a member of the Filipino elite. He was well-educated and generally opposed violence in favor of peaceful reform.[224] Simultaneously, a more radical and secretive nationalist movement emerged, comprised mainly of the lower classes, led by Andres Bonifacio. Neither group could claim a national constituency.[225] As the Spanish began experiencing problems of unrest similar to those they faced in Cuba, they clamped down on security. They arrested

---

[223]David Joel Steinberg, ed., *In Search of Southeast Asia: A Modern History* (Honolulu: University of Hawaii Press, 1985), p. 259. See Steinberg, pp. 259-271, for a discussion of the development of modern nationalism in the Philippines. On the same subject, see also Usha Mahajani, *Philippine Nationalism: External Challenge and Filipino Response, 1565-1946* (St. Lucia: University of Queensland Press, 1971).

[224]Steinberg, p. 261.

[225]Steinberg, pp. 260-261.

Jose Rizal in an attempt to put an end to the civil disorder. The Spanish mistakenly believed that Rizal was the cause of the disorder, and they put him on trial. He was found guilty of inciting insurrection and publicly executed in Manila in 1896.[226]

The Spanish action predictably failed and only served to escalate opposition to their regime, increasing support for the Filipino nationalists. Rizal himself had predicted years earlier that, "the day they (the Spanish) inflict martyrdom... farewell, pro-friar government, and perhaps, farewell Spanish government."[227] By executing Rizal, the Spanish had created a martyr for the two divergent nationalist groups to unite behind. This left Bonifacio as the leader of a broad-based nationalist movement. Anti-Spanish violence increased. However, Bonifacio, a poor general, failed to capitalize on his increased support to win any significant victories against the Spanish.[228] If Bonifacio had been able to do so it certainly would have increased popular support for the nationalist cause.

In the area of Cavite, near Manila, a young man named Emilio Aguinaldo succeeded in winning a major battle against the Spanish. In so doing, he sparked hope into the nationalist movement. Aguinaldo's newly-won prestige

---

[226]Steinberg, p. 261.

[227]Ibid.

[228]Ibid.

led to a power struggle with Bonifacio. Aguinaldo won election as leader of the nationalist movement. He then ordered Bonifacio arrested and tried him for treason in April 1897.[229] Aguinaldo undoubtedly did this to consolidate his power base and to eliminate any potential source of opposition to his leadership. Aguinaldo's court tried Bonifacio for treason and sentenced him to death. Aguinaldo apparently had second thoughts about this decision. He issued a pardon for Bonifacio, but, before it was received by the court, Bonifacio had already been

executed. This left Aguinaldo as the undisputed leader of the nationalists, but the internal power struggle seriously weakened the movement.[230]

In late 1897, the Spanish again clamped down on security in an effort to avoid a prolonged struggle, such as the

Emilio Aguinaldo

---

[229]Steinberg, p. 262.

[230]Ibid.

one they faced in Cuba. In an effort to end the revolt, the Spanish negotiated with Aguinaldo and the nationalists. The result of these negotiations was the truce of Biyak-na-Bato in which Aguinaldo and the rebels received amnesty and 800,000 pesos in exchange for agreeing to voluntary exile.[231] The Spanish felt that they had paid a relatively small price to destroy the opposition without inciting further conflict.[232] Many Filipinos undoubtedly felt that Aguinaldo had sold out their cause. Both sides were wrong. Aguinaldo took the first installment of the Spanish payment, 400,000 pesos, to Hong Kong to buy arms.[233] He then began to organize his nationalist force so that it could seriously challenge the Spanish.

The outbreak of the Spanish-American War in April 1898 provided new hope to Filipino nationalists. Within a week after Congress passed the formal declaration of war against Spain, Admiral George Dewey sought out the Spanish fleet in Manila Bay and destroyed it on May 1, 1898.[234] This represented a dramatic departure from traditional American foreign policy, which had limited its interests mainly to the western hemisphere. It was also a

---

[231]Ibid.; and Petillo, p. 41.

[232]Steinberg, p. 263.

[233]Ibid.; and Petillo, p. 41.

[234]Petillo, p. 39.

complete surprise to the Spanish who had expected the War to be confined to Cuba.

The element of surprise gave Dewey the opportunity to apply the Naval doctrine developed by Alfred T. Mahan, which called for a concentration of force against the enemy fleet. Dewey's defeat of the Spanish in Manila Bay helped justify Mahan's doctrine to the American public. The United States was now reaching outside of the western hemisphere, in a military manner, for the first time. Dewey, however, lacked the manpower to engage the Spanish on land and settled into a naval blockade of Manila while the United States government determined its next move. With their fleet destroyed, the Spanish attempted a series of reforms aimed at regaining the loyalty of the Filipinos, but it was too late.

Dewey facilitated the return of Aguinaldo to the Islands shortly after the naval blockade began. With Aguinaldo's return, the revolution gained new life, receiving support from both the upper and lower classes after Aguinaldo appointed Apolinario Mabini, a prominent member of the upper class, as his chief adviser. Soon, Spanish power was confined to the city of Manila.[235] The nature of the agreement worked out between Aguinaldo and Dewey that resulted in Aguinaldo's return to the Philippines is unclear. Dewey claimed that he had

---

[235]Steinberg, p. 263.

only facilitated Aguinaldo's establishment onshore and provided him with some Mauser rifles. He insisted that he made no agreements with Aguinaldo nor had given him any promises.[236]

According to Dewey, the Filipinos were only interested in bringing an end to Spanish rule and would welcome the Americans if they chose to establish a presence in the Islands.[237] Dewey aided Aguinaldo so that the Spanish would be confronted on land as well as at sea, while the Americans determined their next move. The strategy worked. Soon, the Spanish only retained control of Manila. Aguinaldo claimed that Dewey had assured him that the Americans had no intentions in the Islands beyond the defeat of the Spanish. This led him to declare national independence on June 12, 1898.[238] The United States, meanwhile, was developing an interest in keeping the Islands and did not recognize Aguinaldo's proclamation of Philippine independence. These divergent

---

[236]Brayton Harris, *The Age of the Battleship, 1890-1922* (New York: Franklin Watts, Inc., 1965), pp. 70-71; and George Dewey, *Autobiography of George Dewey, Admiral of the Navy* (New York: Charles Scribner's Sons, 1913). p 247.

[237]Ronald Specter, *Admiral of the New Empire: The Life and Career of George Dewey* (Bacon Rouge: Louisiana State University Press, 1974), p. 86.

[238]Steinberg, p. 263.

courses of action made conflict between the Filipinos and Americans inevitable.

Soon after the War began, the United States started raising troops for service in the Philippines and Cuba. Arthur MacArthur received orders to report to Camp Thomas at Chickamauga, Georgia, to prepare recruits for service in Cuba.[239] MacArthur divided his time between Chickamauga and Tampa, Florida, preparing troops for the war in Cuba. On May 27, 1898, Arthur MacArthur was promoted to Brigadier General of Volunteers.[240] Four days later, on June 1, 1898, MacArthur received new orders. The telegram read:

> You have been confirmed and commission signed by President. Secretary War directs you report General Merritt San Francisco for Duty with expedition for Philippines.[241]

The Army sought out any and all officers with some knowledge of Asia for service in the Philippines. In his report accompanying his request for transfer to China in 1883, MacArthur had demonstrated a far reaching grasp of the situation in the region.

---

[239]Petillo, p. 32; and James, pp 30-31.

[240]*Circulars.*

[241]Manchester, p. 29; and MacArthur, p. 19. Manchester incorrectly states that MacArthur didn't even know where the Philippines was prior to receiving the orders transferring him there.

Before traveling to San
Francisco, MacArthur
returned to Milwaukee for
several days to see his wife
and son.[242] Arthur would
not see Pinky or Douglas
again for three years. On
June 3, 1898, while
MacArthur was in
Milwaukee, the War
Department issued General
Orders No. 63, formally
assigning MacArthur to
General Wesley Merritt in

General Charles King

San Francisco. Along with MacArthur, his long-time friend
Charles King was also made Brigadier General of
Volunteers and assigned to General Merritt.[243] MacArthur
and King left Milwaukee together for San Francisco, where
they arrived on June 12.

Before leaving Milwaukee, Arthur had to restrain
his son Douglas from enlisting and encouraged him to
continue preparing for West Point.[244] Arthur was
more successful with Douglas than his own father had

---

[242]*Charles King Papers*, SHSW.

[243]Ibid.

[244]Manchester, p. 28.

been with him. Douglas continued his preparation for West Point and entered the Military Academy in June 1899.[245] Arthur was well-aware that the Army was changing and that a military education was more important than ever for a successful career.

On June 29, 1898, Arthur MacArthur left San Francisco in charge of the third expedition to the Philippines, with 200 officers and 4,000 men. Accompanying the expedition was Major General Wesley Merritt, who had been appointed commander of the Pacific Theater.[246] MacArthur and his men arrived in Manila Bay on July 31, but bad weather delayed their landing ashore until August 4. The ship was also carrying badly needed ammunition[247] for the troops who had previously arrived in the Philippines to prepare for an assault on Manila.

MacArthur was placed in charge of the first brigade, first division, Eighth Army Corps, with 5,000 men under his

General Wesley Merritt

---

[245]Petillo, p. 32.

[246]Fant, p. 21; and Dewey, p. 272.

[247]Dewey, p. 272.

command.[248] Preparations were made to attack Manila. Two brigades, one commanded by MacArthur and the other by General Francis V. Green, were organized under the command of General Thomas M. Anderson to carry out the attack on the city.[249] Spanish forces in the Philippine capital had been suffering since Aguinaldo, and the Filipino rebels cut off the city's water and food.[250]

Admiral Dewey and Spanish Governor Fermin Juadenes carried on negotiations through the Belgian consul in Manila. The Spanish agreed to surrender the city, but only after they put up a token resistance as a matter of pride. When the Americans attacked the city, the Spanish agreed to offer limited resistance and not to use their artillery. In return, Dewey agreed to keep the artillery of his naval vessels silent and also agreed that the Americans would not allow the Filipino rebels to enter the city.[251]

The battle took place on August 13 and, as agreed, the Spanish quickly surrendered. MacArthur's troops were ordered to circle the city to prevent the Filipino rebels from

---

[248]Leon Wolff, *Little Brown Brother: How the United States Purchased and Pacified the Philippine Islands at the Century's Turn.* (Garden City, NY: Doubleday and Co., Inc., 1961), p. 100.

[249]Fant, p. 25.

[250]Fant, p. 23.

[251]Fant, pp. 22-23.

entering.[252] Aguinaldo, who had been cooperating with the American forces, felt betrayed by the agreement, which kept his forces from joining in the assault on the city.[253] The entire battle had been unnecessary as the Spanish and American governments had agreed to a cessation of hostilities the day before the attack. Orders to this effect were sent to the Philippines,[254] but not received in time to stop the battle.

MacArthur's troops performed brilliantly and suffered minimal casualties in the fighting. Major General Merritt praised MacArthur for "gallantry and excellent judgement."[255] MacArthur was immediately promoted to the rank of Major General of Volunteers and given command of the Second Division, Eighth Army Corps, with 20,000 troops under his command.[256] In addition, MacArthur was named Provost Marshal General of the city of Manila.

---

[252]Wolff, p, 119.

[253]Ibid.; and "Aguinaldo to Anderson, 14 August 1898," in *Correspondence Relating to the War with Spain...* (Washington: U.S. Government Printing Office, 1902), p. 814. Hereafter this source will be cited as *Correspondence*.

[254]"Corbin to Merritt, 12 August 1898," in *Correspondence*, p. 750.

[255]Manchester, p. 29

[256]Circulars; and MacArthur, p. 19.

MacArthur's first act in this capacity was to declare, "this city, its inhabitants, its churches, and religious worship, and its private property of all descriptions are placed under the special safeguard of the faith and honor of the American Army."[257] Aguinaldo continued to hold his position around Manila, while the Americans began fortifying the city's defenses. On August 26, 1898, General Merritt was directed to report to Paris, France, as a member of the Peace Commission to work out the treaty of surrender with the Spanish. Command of overall military operations in the Philippines was turned over to Major General Ewell S. Otis.[258]

The Spanish, the Americans, and the Filipinos all awaited the outcome of the Paris peace talks. On December 10, 1898, the Treaty of Paris ending the Spanish-American War was signed. Article III of the treaty ceded the Philippine Islands to the United States in return for twenty million dollars.[259] The treaty made an already tenuous situation between the Americans and the Filipino rebels even more strained. Aguinaldo began to organize against the Americans as it became clear to him that the result of the War had been to replace one colonial power with another. The Filipinos still held out hope that the treaty

---

[257]Manchester, p. 29; and Wolff, p. 137.

[258]"Corbin to Merritt, 26 August 1898," in *Correspondence*, p. 765.

[259]Wolff, p. 172.

would not be ratified by the United States Senate. Strong anti-imperialist sentiment in the United States made ratification of the treaty uncertain.

In defiance of the Treaty of Paris, Aguinaldo signed a constitution and declared the formation of the Philippine Republic on January 21, 1899.[260] The United States refused to recognize Aguinaldo's government, and tension between the two sides further escalated. Throughout this time, General MacArthur advised General Otis to negotiate with the Filipinos to avoid a conflict. Otis refused any suggestion of discussions with the Filipinos unless they first disarmed.[261] This was not going to happen. All that was needed for hostilities formally to commence was an initial spark. In anticipation of this, the Congress of the newly organized Filipino government voted to give President Aguinaldo the power to declare war whenever he saw fit.[262]

The spark came on February 4, 1899, when skirmishing broke out along the lines north and east of Manila. The circumstances surrounding the outbreak of hostilities are unclear, but the fighting quickly escalated. Aguinaldo attempted a full-scale attack on General MacArthur's troops who were manning the lines. The

---

[260]Steinberg, p. 264.

[261]Manchester, pp. 29-30.

[262]Wolff, p. 206.

formidable defenses that had been erected around the city and the superior American firepower defeated the Filipinos and forced Aguinaldo to abandon his position around the city.[263] Each side blamed the other for initiating the conflict. Two days after the fighting began, the United States Senate ratified the Treaty of Paris by a margin of one vote,[264] committing the United States to a lasting presence in the Philippines. The outbreak of the fighting may actually have helped to provide the necessary votes for ratification as President McKinley reported to the Senate that the Filipinos had instigated the fighting.

From February to November 1899, the American Army, led by General MacArthur in the field, pursued the Filipino Army northward from Manila. General Otis, overall commander of American forces in the Philippines, directed operations from Manila. Otis behaved much the same way his Spanish predecessors had, refusing to leave Manila to observe the conditions in the countryside. Otis was an inept leader, so it was probably best for the Army that he did not take command in the field.

The War became one between the "Goddamns," as the Americans referred to themselves and the "Gugus," as

---

[263]James, p. 32.

[264]David Haward Bain, *Sitting in Darkness: Americans in the Philippines* (Boston: Houghton Mifflin Co. 1984), p. 79; and Steinberg, p. 265.

American soldiers with natives in the Philippines

they referred to the Filipinos.[265] It would be a bitter drawn-out war filled with ugly displays of racist attitudes by many Americans and with both sides committing atrocities against the other. The Americans also referred to the Filipinos as "Niggers." Such racist attitudes generated resentment from African-American soldiers who were not treated as equals by many of their white counterparts. The Filipinos tried to capitalize on this resentment by using propaganda to entice black soldiers to join their cause. Such Filipino efforts generally failed as no more than a dozen African-American soldiers deserted to join the insurgents.[266] Black soldiers rarely displayed any racist

---

[265]Manchester, p. 30.

[266]Willard B. Gatewood Jr., *Black Americans and the White Man's Burden 1898-1903* (Urbana, IL: University of Illinois Press, 1975),

attitudes toward the Filipinos. Because of this, they usually enjoyed better relations with the native population.[267] Despite the difficulties they faced, African-American soldiers were widely praised for their performance in battle.[268] General MacArthur worked hard to restrain racist attitudes on the part of his troops and did not allow such attitudes to affect his dealings with the troops under his command or with the Filipinos.

In March 1899, General Otis ordered an attack upon the Filipino capital of Malolos. Malolos had served as the rebel capital since Aguinaldo had proclaimed the Filipino Republic the summer before. Applying traditional military strategy in an untraditional situation, Otis reasoned that the capture of the rebel capital would compel the Filipinos to surrender and submit to American authority. The city was attacked on March 30, but Aguinaldo, who had realized that his position in Malolos had become indefensible, evacuated the city under cover of darkness the night before the American attack. Aguinaldo left a small detachment to offer token resistance and cover the

---

p. 287. This book is an authoritative study of the role of the African-American soldiers in the Philippines.

[267]Gatewood, p. 279.

[268]Gatewood, p. 275.

retreat.[269] Otis' unrealistic hopes were dashed and the war continued.

Like many other American military commanders, Otis believed that the Filipinos would welcome American rule and that Aguinaldo and his rebels represented only a small minority of the native population. In his reports back to Washington, Otis continually insisted that the war was nearing a conclusion.[270]

MacArthur never agreed with Otis' policies toward the rebels. He quickly realized that the war would be a costly, long, drawn-out struggle because the Filipinos were united in their opposition to the Americans. This viewpoint brought him into continual conflict with Otis.[271] Otis' indecision and attitude about the nature of the war led MacArthur to exclaim, "Otis is a locomotive bottom side up, with the wheels revolving at full speed."[272] MacArthur viewed the desire of the Filipinos for independence as natural and legitimate. He also

---

[269]Richard E. Nelch Jr., *Response to Imperialism: The United States and the Philippine-American War, 1899-1902* (Chapel Hill: The University of North Carolina Press, 1979), p. 26.

[270]Wolff, p. 310.

[271]Ibid.

[272]Lee and Henschel, p. 19; and James, p. 35.

recognized that Aguinaldo was the key figure in a national movement.[273]

The War progressed slowly throughout the heat of summer. In April, General Charles King was sent home to the United States on account of illness.[274] The main American offensive against the Filipino insurgents was launched in November 1899. The plan called for the American force to divide into three groups. The main body of the Army, led by MacArthur, was to attack Aguinaldo, then at Tarlac, and pursue him northward to the mountains. The second group, under General Henry W. Lawton, was to move northward and close off Aguinaldo's escape routes into the Caraballo and Sierra Madre Mountains. The third group, commanded by General Lloyd Wheaton, was to sail from Manila to the Gulf of Lingayen and march inland to close off mountain passes to the north. If all went according to plan, Aguinaldo would be trapped and either compelled to surrender or be destroyed.

---

[273]Welch, P. 35.

[274]*Charles King Papers*, SHSW; and Charles King Collection, Milwaukee County Historical Society; and *Diary of Brigadier General Charles King during the Philippine Insurrection. June 11, 1898 to February 5, 1899*, Wis. Mss. KW (Micro 257), State Historical Society of Wisconsin. King's diary is an interesting account of his experiences in the Philippines from when he was ordered there until the outbreak of the insurrection.

MacArthur commanding his troops in the Philippines

Things did not work out as planned. When the offensive launched in early November, MacArthur's force carried out its role brilliantly. His troops advanced by echelon from one flank to the other, continually driving the rebels northward. General Lawton's force reached its position in accordance with the plan and sealed off Aguinaldo's escape routes into the mountain passes in the northeast. General Wheaton's force, however, failed to reach its planned position, and Aguinaldo and the Filipinos beat him to the Tila Pass, near Pozorrubio, and escaped into the mountains.[275]

The Filipinos were badly beaten, but not destroyed. Otis believed this victory marked the end of the war, but MacArthur realized that a new war was now set to begin.[276] Aguinaldo disbanded his Army and planned to wage a guerilla war against the Americans.[277] In an effort to weaken the guerilla movement before it got organized, MacArthur recommended to Otis that an amnesty be

---

[275]*Five Years of the War Department Following the War with Spain, 1899-1901, As Shown in the Reports of the Secretary of War* (Washington: U.S. Government Printing Office, 1904), pp. 13-14. This source is hereafter cited as *Five Years of the War Department*; and Welch, p. 32; and MacArthur, p. 21; and James, p. 33.

[276]Gatewood, p. 261, incorrectly states that MacArthur was one of those who believed the war was over with the conclusion of the November offensive.

[277]Welch, p. Z5.

offered to all rebels who surrendered and that thirty pesos be given for each rifle that was turned over. Otis rejected this plan,[278] believing the rebels were a band of outlaws who should be treated as criminals and that the war was now rapidly approaching its conclusion.

MacArthur was one of the few who realized that a deadlier war was about to begin. In December, Aguinaldo disbanded the rebel Army as he realized the Filipinos could not accomplish their objectives through conventional warfare. The Filipino rebels explained, "The object of guerilla warfare is to show them their mistake: until they recognize our rights to independence, there shall be no rest for our unfortunate people, who shall never cease hostilities against the ambitious invader, making rest impossible for him."[279] The Filipinos intended to keep up guerilla warfare indefinitely until the Americans tired of the war and granted the Filipinos independence. The rebel Army dissolved into small bands that would operate independently on a local basis. The command structure of

---

[278]James, p. 35.

[279]*Annual Reports of the War Department for the Fiscal Year Ended June 30, 1900: Report of the Lieutenant General Commanding the Army*, Part 3 (Washington: U.S. Government Printing Office, 1900), p. 72. This contains the report of the Military Governor of the Philippines. Appendix I, attached to MacArthur's report is a translation of a pamphlet published by the Filipino Revolutionary Committee, which explains their objectives in pursuing guerilla warfare and the tactics used (see pp. 72-76).

the force was maintained, but it now operated in a much more informal manner and became highly secretive.[280]

On January 2, 1900, Arthur MacArthur was promoted to the permanent rank of Brigadier General.[281] 1900 was an election year and the debate over the role of the United States in the Philippine Islands was one of the key issues in the presidential campaign.[282] The McKinley Administration wanted to portray to the American public that the war in the Philippines was winding down and that the process of Americanizing the Filipinos could begin. General Otis' reports to Washington had supported this view.

In early April 1900, General Otis requested that he be relieved of command in the Philippines as private interests required his presence in the United States.[283] Otis' request was honored, and he turned over command to General Arthur MacArthur in accordance with instructions from

---

[280]Welch, p. 25.

[281]*Circulars.* The rank of Major General of Volunteers, which MacArthur had held, was a temporary rank for the specific action and did not alter his permanent rank of Lieutenant Colonel. Now, MacArthur was promoted to the permanent rank of Brigadier General.

[282]Paul F. Boller, *Presidential Campaigns* (New York: Oxford University Press, 1984), p. 181.

[283]"Otis to Adjutant General, 3 April 1900," in *Correspondence*, p. 1156.

the Secretary of War. MacArthur was ordered to spend the month before Otis' departure traveling throughout the Philippines to ascertain the overall situation.[284] The change of command worked well with the Administration's strategy to portray a normalizing situation in the Philippines. Otis was brought home amidst much fanfare and given the welcome of a conquering hero.[285]

Arthur MacArthur received the title of Military Governor and assumed command in the Philippines on May 5, 1900.[286] The creation of the post of Military Governor was in itself an attempt to portray a normalizing situation in the Philippines. It suggested that the groundwork for a government was being established.

MacArthur was an extremely skilled officer and far better suited to a military command than Otis. MacArthur understood the nature of the Filipino resistance. He had faced guerilla warfare in Tennessee during the Civil War, and his previous combat experience proved invaluable. Otis, on the other hand, did not understand guerilla warfare.[287] MacArthur performed his new duties

---

[284]"Corbin to Otis, 4, 8 April 1900," in *Correspondence*, p. 1157.

[285]Stuart Creighton Miller, *Benevolent Assimilation: The American Conquest of the Philippines, 1899-1903* (New Haven: Yale University Press, 1982), pp. 100-102.

[286]*Circulars*; and Wolff, p. 310.

[287]Wolff, p. 310.

diligently. Always the student, as he had demonstrated time and again during his days on the western frontier, MacArthur spent every available moment studying, seeking out every book on the far east that was available.[288]

In February 1900, President McKinley announced the formation of a second Philippine Commission headed by Judge William Howard Taft. The work of this commission, unlike the first Philippine Commission that had largely served to gather information on the situation in the Islands, was to help bring about the gradual transfer of power in the Philippines from military to civilian rule.[289] The creation of this commission also helped to reinforce the McKinley administration's narrative of a normalizing situation in the Philippines. The Administration did not want to allow the Democrats and anti-imperialists to claim that the situation in the Philippines was precarious with the election soon approaching. Others named to the second Philippine Commission were Dean Worchester, who had

---

[288]James, p. 40, and Manchester, p. 32

[289]Dean C. Worchester, *The Philippines Past and Present* (New York: The MacMillan Company, 1930), p. 269; and Ralph E. Minger, "Taft, MacArthur, and the Establishment of Civil Government in the Philippines" in *The Ohio Historical Quarterly*, 70 (1961), p. 310. Minger has done the best work on the Taft-MacArthur conflict in the Philippines, but he has a slight bias in favor of Taft and relies too much on Taft's personal papers to tell the story without consideration of MacArthur's viewpoint.

served on the first Philippine Commission, Luke E. Wright, Henry C. Ide, and Bernard Moses.[290]

Unlike his predecessor, Arthur MacArthur was greatly respected by the men who served under him. A strong and determined leader, General MacArthur had gained the respect of his subordinates by his sound judgement. He was also not afraid to lead his men in battle. Many of the most prominent American military figures of the next generation received their training under MacArthur in the Philippines. Among them: William "Billy" Mitchell, whose father, John Mitchell, had served alongside MacArthur in the 24th Wisconsin during the Civil War;[291] Peyton March, who became Chief of Staff of the Army during World War I; John J. "Black Jack" Pershing of World War I fame;[292] Frederick Funston, who would achieve fame in the Philippines, as well as later in

---

[290]Worchester, p. 269.

[291]For MacArthur's relationship to Mitchell, see *General William Mitchell Correspondence 1888, 1893-1904, 1927 (restricted)*. Micro 293, State Historical Society of Wisconsin; and *MacArthurs of Milwaukee*, pp. 49-50.

[292]Evidence of MacArthur's relationship with Pershing can be found in Frank E. Vandiver, *Black Jack: The Life and Times of John J. Pershing*, 2 vols. (College Station: Texas A&H University Press, 1977). In 1903, while in California, Pershing made a special point of paying a visit to MacArthur (p. 324).

his military career;[293] Enoch Crowder, MacArthur's
secretary and legal advisor who later became Judge
Advocate General of the Army;[294] and J. Franklin Bell and
Charles P. Sumerall, each of whom later served as Chief of
Staff of the Army.[295]

On June 3, 1900 the Second Philippine Commission
headed by William Howard Taft, arrived in Manila Bay.
The Commission received a cool reception from
MacArthur, who sent his aide, Enoch Crowder, to greet the
commissioners.[296] MacArthur referred to the Commission

---

[293]MacArthur's close relationship with Funston is evidenced in
Frederick Funston, *Memories of Two Wars: Cuban and Philippine
Experiences* (New York: Charles Scribner's Sons, 1911). MacArthur
recommended Funston for the Medal of Honor while he served
under him in the Philippines (p. 289). Funston also named his son
after MacArthur, Arthur MacArthur Funston, indicating the great
respect he accorded MacArthur (see the dedication in Funston's
book).

[294]Manchester, p. 30. Crowder famously said of MacArthur,
"Arthur MacArthur as the most flamboyantly egotistical man I had
ever seen, until I met his son." Although MacArthur and Crowder
worked closely together, their relationship was not particularly
close. Crowder's statement is misleading because MacArthur was
actually a very reserved man.

[295]James, pp. 35-36.

[296]James, p. 37; and Minger, p. 313.

as "an injection into an otherwise normal situation."[297] Mac-Arthur felt that the Commission infring-ed upon his authority as Military Governor. The fact that MacArthur and Taft had very different ideas about American policy in the Philippines made matters even more difficult. These differences of opinion, combined with disputes over jurisdiction, made conflict between the two men inevitable. According to the directive establishing the Commission, the Military Governor would continue to serve as Chief Executive and would have control over both military and civil operations in the Philippines. The Commission, beginning on September 1, would have legislative functions and would appropriate funds and appoint civilian offi-cials.[298]

Two days after the arrival of the Commission, Mac-Arthur wired Washington asking for approval to implement the amnesty proposal that he had originally suggested to Otis. President McKinley approved

---

[297]Peter W. Stanley, *A Nation in the Making: The Philippines and the United States, 1899-1921* (Cambridge: Harvard University Press, 1974), p. 77; and Wolff, p. 312.

[298]Rowland Tappan Bertoff, "Taft and MacArthur, 1900; A Study in Civil-Military Relations," in *World Politics: A Quarterly Journal of International Relations*, 5 (1953), p. 196. Like Minger, Bertoff's work is biased toward Taft in relation to the conflict with MacArthur and relies too heavily upon Taft's personal correspondence.

MacArthur's plan the following day.[299] On June 21, 1900, MacArthur formally issued an offer of amnesty to any Filipino rebel who would sign an oath of allegiance to the United States, provided that they had not violated the laws of war. In addition, thirty pesos would be given for any rifle in good condition that was turned in when surrendering.[300] The amnesty was offer was extended for a ninety-day period. After that time, any Filipino who failed to assist the American Army would be held suspect.

The amnesty offer proved unsuccessful. Aguinaldo rejected it, and few Filipinos actually surrendered.[301] Of those who did, only one in twenty was carrying a rifle. The condition that excluded those who had violated the laws of war was vaguely worded. Many rebels feared that when they surrendered, they would face harsh punishment from the Americans. Other Filipinos feared retaliation from their own countrymen who would naturally view their surrender as an act of treason. Perhaps the most significant reason for the failure of MacArthur's amnesty offer was that the Filipinos still had hope of ultimately achieving victory, especially if William Jennings Bryan and the

---

[299]"MacArthur to Adjutant General, 5 June 1900," and "Corbin to MacArthur, 6 June 1900," in *Correspondence*, p. 1175.

[300]Welch, p. 35; and *Annual Reports*, 1900, p. 65 for the entire text of MacArthur's proclamation.

[301]Annual Reports, 1900, p. 66. 5,022 persons surrendered as a result of MacArthur's amnesty offer.

Democrats defeated William McKinley and the Republicans in the November election.[302] Bryan and the Democrats favored granting Philippine independence as soon as possible.[303]

MacArthur's purpose in making the amnesty offer was to undermine the nationalist movement. Despite its failure, he continued to pursue other policies designed to weaken the resistance. MacArthur had no illusions that these were anything but long term measures to pacify the population. Ultimately, he believed that this would be the only way to bring about a lasting peace. MacArthur encouraged the building of schools, which in 1900, enrolled 100,000 Filipino children.[304] MacArthur also established civil courts, introduced the writ of habeas corpus, set up a tariff system designed to bolster the Filipino economy, and put the Filipino currency on the gold standard. MacArthur also encouraged the building of hospitals and established a Philippine Supreme Court with

---

[302]Miller, p. 148; and Welch, p. 35.

[303]Boller, p. 181.

[304]Annual Reports of the War Department for the Fiscal Year Ended June 30, 1900: Report of the Military Governor of the Philippine Islands on Civil Affairs (Washington: U.S. Government Printing Office, 1900), p. 26

a membership comprised of six Filipinos and three American officers.[305]

The immediate impact of these measures was negligible. Still, they contributed to gradually breaking up the alliance between upper and lower class Filipinos that had been so important to Aguinaldo's success.[306] In this regard, these measures contributed significantly to the collapse of the Philippine rebellion. These pacification policies were also important in the long term in helping to maintain peace in the Islands by providing benefits to the population that they had not known under their Spanish conquerors.

Another of MacArthur's policies was to establish the Philippine Scouts as a branch of the United States Army.[307] The Scouts were a small military force trained by American officers. In all, fewer than five thousand Filipinos served in this outfit during the Philippine Insurrection.[308] Most of those who did were from upper class families, who had traditionally cooperated with the Spanish.[309] The Philippine Scouts would eventually play

---

[305]Pomeroy, p. 141; and MacArthur, p. 24; and Stanley, p. 81.

[306]Steinberg, p. 265.

[307]MacArthur, p. 24.

[308]Miller, p. 269.

[309]Miller, p. 81.

an important role in bringing about an end to the revolution.

In the summer of 1900, the Boxer Rebellion broke out in China. MacArthur received orders from Washington to send troops to China as part of an expeditionary force to deal with the rebellion. In June, MacArthur, in compliance with orders from Washington, sent one regiment to China. He firmly opposed additional withdrawals on the grounds that they would seriously jeopardize the situation in the Philippines,[310] which required a great deal of manpower due to the nature of guerrilla warfare. At this time, MacArthur was commanding a force of over sixty thousand men.[311]

In July 1900, MacArthur requested that he be sent to China to direct the field operations of the American Expeditionary Force. MacArthur's request was denied and General Adna Chaffee was sent to command the American force.[312] From the moment the Second Philippine Commission arrived in the Islands, MacArthur felt that it impinged upon his authority. He preferred not to operate

---

[310]William Reynolds Braisted, *The United States Navy in the Pacific, 1897-1909* (New York: Greenwood Press, Publishers, 1969), p. 106; and D. Challener, *Admirals, Generals, and American Foreign Policy; 1898-1914* (Princeton: Princeton University Press, 1973), p. 200.

[311]Ganoe, p. 407.

[312]James, p. 37.

under these conditions and felt he would be better suited to a field command. Arthur's son, Arthur III, had been serving in the Navy and was also stationed in the Philippines. He was sent with the naval force from the Philippines to China to deal with the Boxer Rebellion.[313]

In September 1900, the Second Philippine Commission began exercising its official duties. These responsibilities, MacArthur had been assured by Secretary of War Elihu Root, in no way infringed upon the authority he exercised as Military Governor. The Administration had never clearly defined the relationship between MacArthur and the Commission to the satisfaction of either party.[314] With the election rapidly approaching, the McKinley Administration desperately wanted to give the American public the impression of a normalizing situation in the Philippines. The Commission played an important role in helping them accomplish this, but it also set the stage for a power struggle to develop between MacArthur and William Howard Taft. This struggle would ultimately determine the direction of American policy in the Philippine Islands.

William Howard Taft was an obese man, weighing well in excess of three hundred pounds. Though Taft was Yale-educated and had been a successful lawyer and

---

[313]MacArthur, p. 17.

[314]see Minger and Bertoff for more information on this.

William Howard Taft

judge, he was unprepared for his new assignment. Taft knew very little about the Philippines before he arrived in the Islands. Nevertheless, he possessed some very strong ideas about what America's role there should be.[315] Taft believed that the United States should have established a civilian government in the Philippines immediately after the Spanish surrender. Had this been done, Taft felt that there would have been no insurrection and that the Filipinos would have happily and willingly accepted American rule.[316] He adopted a very patronizing attitude toward the Filipinos, referring to them as "Our Little Brown Brothers."[317] This attitude was insulting to Filipinos

---

[315]Minger, pp. 309-310.

[316]Mahajani, p. 235.

[317]Wolff, p. 313.

whom Taft saw as grown-up children, lacking in moral character.[318] Taft's attitude also drew scorn from many American soldiers, who, for reasons of racial prejudice and the fact that they were being shot and killed by Filipinos, found it hard to accept them as their brothers. The soldiers developed a song ridiculing Taft's attitude:

> *I'm only a common soldier in the blasted Philippines.*
> *They say I've got brown brothers here, but I dunno what*
> *it means.*
> *I like the word fraternity, but still I draw the line.*
> *He may be a brother of Big Bill Taft,*
> *But he ain't no brother of mine![319]*

Taft rationalized, much like General Otis before him, that a small insignificant tribal faction led the Filipino resistance to the Americans, using terror tactics to keep the large majority of Filipinos from embracing American rule.[320] With a heated debate over the American presence in the Islands going on in the United States prior to the presidential election, Taft believed that many Filipinos feared that the United States would withdraw from the Islands if Bryan was elected, leaving them to face the wrath

---

[318]Minger, p. 316; and Mahajani, p. 235.

[319]Wolff, p. 313.

[320]Stanley, p. 65.

of Aguinaldo and his band of outlaws who would take vengeance upon them.[321]

Taft adopted the slogan, "The Philippines for the Filipinos," but in reality, he was imbued with the ideology of a traditional colonialist. Taft believed that the role of the United States in the Philippines should be a permanent one. He believed in colonies as a source for raw materials and as a market for exports. With this in mind, Taft ridiculed the Army's role in suppressing the Philippine Insurrection:

> If business is going to succeed here, it must be in the sale of American goods to the eight million Filipinos. One would think that a child in business might understand that the worst possible policy in attempting to sell goods is to abuse, berate, and vilify your only possible customers.[322]

Taft's entire outlook on the situation in the Philippines was naive. He believed that military action was unnecessary and only served to prevent the Filipinos from joyfully embracing American rule. Taft harshly criticized MacArthur for censoring news releases, despite the fact that the orders for censorship emanated from the Secretary of War.[323] Censorship in the Philippines had not been

---

[321]Stanley, p. 78.

[322]Wolff, p. 313.

[323]Miller, p. 135.

initiated under MacArthur. His predecessor, General Otis, had maintained strict censorship of news reports coming from the Philippines to ensure that they portrayed the situation favorably.[324] This was all done in accordance with the Administration's practice of portraying a normalizing situation in the Philippines.

Taft's main criticism of MacArthur was of the zealous nature of his censorship policies which Taft called revolting and un-American.[325] MacArthur believed that censorship was a military necessity so as not to give the Filipino resistance any ammunition for propaganda, which might enhance their popular support. Taft's outlook was based on the premise that, "a great majority of the people long for peace and would be entirely willing to accept the establishment of a government under the supremacy of the United States were it not for their fear of the insurrectos."[326] Taft in effect saw the Filipinos as little children in need of guidance and supervision from their big brother Uncle Sam, or in this case, Big Bill. He insulted the Filipinos' intelligence and could not see their desire for independence as natural or legitimate.[327] Taft failed to understand the concept of nationalism, which had been at

---

[324]Bain, p. B3.

[325]Minger, p. 318.

[326]Stanley, p. 78.

[327]Mahajani, p. 235.

work in the Philippines prior to the American involvement there.

MacArthur, on the other hand, saw the Filipinos as a proud and intelligent people with a legitimate desire for independence. He realized that the United States was engaged in conquering an entire population[328] and not merely out to defeat a band of outlaws. MacArthur did not see the American role in the Philippines as a permanent one. MacArthur saw the American purpose as being to strengthen the Philippines and prepare them for independence so that they would not fall prey to one of the other colonial powers. MacArthur preferred to refer to the Philippines as a tuitionate that the United States was preparing for self-government,[329] and which would become a strong ally of the United States. Taft recognized this and wrote in horror to Secretary of War Elihu Root that, "MacArthur has some very definite views which he once expressed to me that we are here only to prepare these people for independence."[330] MacArthur saw the Filipino desire for independence as natural, and he took the extent and intensity of the Filipino resistance to the

---

[328]Lee and Henschel, p. 22.

[329]Petillo, p. 96.

[330]Stanley, p. 79.

Americans seriously. MacArthur regarded the Filipinos as a proud people refusing to accept subjugation.[331]

MacArthur warned in his annual report, in September 1900, that the war was not winding down and that the rebels enjoyed widespread support among the general population.[332] This portrayal of the Philippine situation met with skepticism at the White House because both Otis and Taft had expressed quite different views from those of MacArthur.[333]

MacArthur realized that the Americans were fighting an entire population and not merely a band of outlaws. With this in mind, he knew that the Americans would have to resort to total war tactics to bring an end to the insurrection. MacArthur explained in his report that:

> Wherever, throughout the archipelago, there is a group of the insurgent army, it is a fact, beyond dispute, that all towns contribute to the maintenance thereof. In other words, the towns, regardless of the fact of American occupation and town organization,

---

[331]Mahajani, p. 235.

[332]*Annual Reports*, 1900.

[333]Margaret Leech, *In the Days of McKinley* (New York: Harper and Brothers Publishers, 1959), p. 571.

are the actual bases for all insurgent military activity.[334]

MacArthur realized that guerilla warfare did not merely involve small bands acting independently, but, instead, it was a highly organized systematic activity involving an entire population. This is further demonstrated by the Filipino guerrilla warfare tactics manual, which stated:

> We say again that a guerilla warfare is easy to sustain and keep up indefinitely, all the pueblos protecting, of course, our guerrillas, who are only defending the common cause...[335]

MacArthur went on to explain in his report for 1900 that:

> The success of this unique system of war depends upon almost complete unity of action of the entire native population. That such unity is a fact is too obvious to admit discussion; how it is brought about and maintained is not so plain. Intimidation has undoubtedly accomplished much to this end, but fear as the only motive is hardly sufficient to account for the united and apparently spontaneous action of several millions of people. One traitor in each town would effectually destroy such a complex

---

[334]*Annual Reports*, 1900, p. 61.

[335]*Annual Reports*, 1900, p. 73.

organization. It is probable that the adhesive principle comes from ethnological homogeneity which induces men to respond for a time to the appeals of consanguineous leadership, even when such action is opposed to their own interests and convictions of expediency.[336]

MacArthur's report certainly did not conform to the Administration's goal of portraying a normalizing situation in the Philippines. The McKinley Administration decided not to make the report public until after the November election so as not to give the anti-imperialist forces a rallying point from which to attack McKinley's foreign policy. When the report was finally made public, the Administration's decision not to release it prior to the election was heavily criticized by the press.[337]

The McKinley Administration's policy was successful inasmuch as the President was re-elected by the largest margin of victory since the election of 1872.[338] This victory was not necessarily a mandate for American involvement in the Philippines as the election had hinged on a variety of issues. Nevertheless, Republicans and imperialists hailed it as a public mandate for the President's foreign

---

[336]*Annual Reports*, 1900, p. 62.

[337]Miller, p. 150.

[338]Boller, p. 181.

policy.[339] The election made certain that American involvement in the Philippine Islands would continue.

With the election now over, the time had come for the Americans to take decisive action to end the Filipino resistance. Discouraged by the results of the election of 1900, the Filipinos began to realize that the Americans would not voluntarily leave the Islands anytime soon. To affect the large scale pacification necessary to end the insurrection, the Army was reinforced to its peak strength in the Islands of 75,000 men.[340] MacArthur now commanded the largest force under any American General since the Civil War.

On December 20, 1900, MacArthur issued a proclamation placing the Islands under martial law.[341] Several Filipino POWs were executed for having killed American prisoners of war, and many others were deported to Guam for having committed atrocities.[342] Any towns found supporting the insurgency would be occupied, and any civilian found to be aiding the rebels would be imprisoned.[343] In villages found to be aiding the

---

[339]Ibid

[340]Wolff, p. 334.

[341]Ibid.; and Bain, p. 203; and *Five Years of the War Department*, p. 173

[342]*Five Years of the War Department*, p. 173.

[343]Miller, p. 153.

rebel resistance, the population in and around the town was rounded up into what amounted to prisons under the guard of American soldiers. The War Department expressed some concern over this policy, which was under the supervision of Major Fred A. Smith, but MacArthur reassured Washington that, "His action effectively suppressing insurrection there which the past three months had presented obstinate resistance. Exclusively a military measure carried out without objectionable or offensive features and effected end in view."[344] As the Filipino population began to fear American retaliation, support for the resistance gradually weakened, but victory for the Americans was still a long way off.

Despite the harsh nature of these pacification policies, MacArthur worked hard to restrain racism and atrocities committed by American soldiers against the captured guerillas, as well as the civilian population.[345] Taft was disillusioned because the result of the presidential election seemed to have had very little impact on ending the Filipino resistance. Taft had chastised MacArthur in the past for being too brutal in his dealings with the Filipinos. Speaking of MacArthur, Taft said, "I have no doubt that he

---

[344]Miller, p. 208; and "MacArthur to Adjutant General, 22 March 1901," in *Correspondence*, p. 1261.

[345]Bertoff, p. 199.

is a good soldier, but his experience and his ability as a statesman or politician are nothing."[346]

Now Taft began to criticize MacArthur for being too lenient with the Filipino rebels. Taft referred to the insurgents as "terrorists and assassins" and called on MacArthur to implement more deportations and executions. Taft continued to believe that the rebels were responsible for preventing the Filipino people from embracing American rule. Despite Taft's criticisms, MacArthur still sought peace with the insurgents and respected them as soldiers. MacArthur pardoned those who surrendered and refused to confiscate their property. Deportations were used mainly for criminal offenders.[347]

MacArthur always accorded the Filipino insurgents the respect that his military code bound him to. Taft did not understand this military code of ethics and wrote to Secretary of War Root, criticizing MacArthur. The future President and Chief Justice declared that it is necessary "to depart from this policy of leniency which up to this time has been pursued by the American forces and authorities, and give the men in arms an opportunity to come in, and if they don't accept it, declare them outlaws and either hang or transport them as they are captured. This is entirely justified.... The resistance to American authority is

---

[346]Minger, p. 321.

[347]Stanley, pp. 65-66.

nothing but a conspiracy of murder and assassination."[348] Taft's ignorance of Philippine nationalism remained evident. MacArthur felt that executions and deportations were only justified in cases where war crimes were committed and not as punishment for opposing American rule.[349]

In January 1901, Army Intelligence turned up documents implicating a Japanese Consular in Manila of encouraging and aiding the Filipino resistance movement. Arthur recognized the threat posed by Japan to the American position in the Philippines and forwarded the documents to the Adjutant General. MacArthur reported:

> The conclusion arising from a perusal of these papers is almost irresistible that Japanese interference is one of the elements sustaining the insurrection in these islands. What force is to be attributed to it is not yet apparent, but it is believed that the hostile attitude of the Japanese and possibly the Japanese government itself demands the closest consideration by our government in Washington.[350]

---

[348]Stanley, p. 65.

[349]Stanley, pp. 65-66.

[350]Challener, pp. 228-229.

This was a threat that Arthur's son Douglas failed to give enough emphasis to in the time preceding the Japanese invasion of the Philippines in World War II.

On February 5, 1901, Arthur MacArthur was promoted to the permanent rank of Major General.[351] The total war policy which had been applied by MacArthur, up to this point, had successfully undercut some of the support for Aguinaldo and the rebels. Still, it had not done enough to seriously damage the insurgent's cause. MacArthur's policies sought to divide the Filipino rebels in hopes that the upper class would gradually resign itself to accept American rule and reap the benefits it offered them.

MacArthur realized, from his early days in the Islands, that Aguinaldo was the thread holding the Filipino resistance together.[352] The Army, however, had been unsuccessful in ascertaining where Aguinaldo was hiding and directing the opposition from since the beginning of the guerilla war at the end of 1899. Finally, in February 1901, the opportunity presented itself when Aguinaldo's personal courier, Cecilio Segismundo, was captured and interrogated by General Frederick Funston, commander of the sector where he was apprehended. Segismundo told

---

[351]Circulars.

[352]Bain, p. 13; and William F. Zornow, "Funston Captures Aguinaldo," in *American Heritage*, 9 (February 1958), p. 25.

Funston that Aguinaldo's headquarters was in Palinan, in Isabella Province, and the documents that he was carrying convinced Funston that the information he provided was correct.[353]

Funston traveled to Manila to see MacArthur at Malacañang Palace.[354] They devised an elaborate plan whereby Funston, accompanied by four other Americans, Segismundo, and a group of the Philippine Scouts, would land at Casiguran Bay and proceed inland to Aguinaldo's headquarters. Using forged papers, the Scouts claimed to be insurgents who were taking their American prisoners to Aguinaldo for interrogation. If all went according to plan, they would then capture Aguinaldo and return with him to Manila.[355] Before Funston departed from Manila, MacArthur said to him, "Funston, this is a desperate undertaking. I fear I shall never see you again."[356]

MacArthur saw this as a desperate mission because he realized that only the capture of Aguinaldo could bring a swift end to the insurgency. The operation commenced on

---

[353]Welch, p. 37; and Zornow, p. 26.

[354]Bain, p. 204. Malacañang Palace was the former residence of the Spanish Governor before becoming American headquarters in Manila. It now serves as the Presidential Palace.

[355]Saswolff, p. 342. See Zornow and Bain for detailed accounts of Funston's mission to capture Aguinaldo.

[356]Bain, p. 210; and Zornow, p. 27.

February 14, 1901. Funston and his men went inland 100 miles from Casiguran Bay to Palinan, successfully captured Aguinaldo, and returned safely with him to the coast all in six weeks.[357] Early on the morning of March 28, 1901, Funston arrived at Malacañang Palace and informed MacArthur of Aguinaldo's presence there. The three men sat down to breakfast. Aguinaldo was understandably nervous, but MacArthur soon put him at ease by sending for his wife and children whom he had not seen since the early days of the war.[358] MacArthur treated Aguinaldo courteously and accorded him the dignity and respect of a fellow officer, ignoring calls by Taft and others for his deportation or execution.[359]

On April 1, Aguinaldo formally surrendered and signed an oath of allegiance to the United States. On April 19, Aguinaldo issued an address to the Filipino people calling for an end to the resistance to the Americans.[360] He was kept under house arrest in Manila until July 4, 1902, when President Theodore Roosevelt officially declared the Philippine Insurrection to be over.[361] Aguinaldo's surrender was the death blow for the Philippine Uprising.

---

[357]Wolff, p. 342.

[358]Funston, p. 425; and Bain, p. 383.

[359]Stanley, p. 79; and Bain, p. 384.

[360]Stanley, p. 79; and Bain, p. 385.

[361]Bain, p. 385.

It removed the stigma of treason from the act, and gradually, rebel armies put down their arms. Another year would pass before the insurrection would officially be over, but the end was now in sight, and the outcome no longer in doubt.

This success provided great relief to the government in Washington, which had been claiming the rebellion was nearing its conclusion since early 1900. MacArthur sought permission from Washington to reinstate his amnesty offer. He believed that, combined with Aguinaldo's surrender, it would effectively end the resistance to American rule, but Washington refused.[362] Prior to Aguinaldo's capture, Washington had been making plans for a transfer from military to civilian rule in the Philippines.

At the heart of the dispute between Taft and MacArthur was the latter's understanding that the President's right to appoint governing officials in the Philippines emanated from his constitutional power as Commander-in-Chief of the armed forces. Therefore, he concluded that presidential authority did not allow him to appoint civilians to official posts in the Islands.[363] MacArthur believed that the Commission was an

---

[362]"MacArthur to Adjutant General, 10 April 1901," and "Corbin to MacArthur, 11 April 1901," in *Correspondence*, pp. 1267-1268.

[363]Petillo, *Dissertation*, p. 103; and Minger, p. 326.

unconstitutional interference with his authority as Military Governor, and he seldom consulted the commission, except in cases where the responsibilities were clearly legislative.[364] Taft was extremely critical of MacArthur's views in this regard and wrote:

> It has always been a curious phase of political human nature to me to observe that men who have not had the slightest knowledge of legal principles and do not claim to have had any legal education feel entirely at home in the construction of the constitution and in using its limitations to support their views and to nullify action, the wisdom of which they dispute. The constitution has not often been used to maintain undiminished the absolute legislative, executive, and judicial power of a subordinate military commander as against the express orders of his constitutional commander in chief.[365]

Taft was wrong in his assessment of MacArthur. The General had studied law and had even received a degree from the National University. MacArthur was a strong-willed individual who would take issue with his Commander-in-Chief if his orders violated the constitution. MacArthur's maxim, which he probably learned from his Civil War days, was "Sometimes one has

---

[364]Bertoff, p. 206.

[365]Minger, p. 327.

to decide for oneself the relevancy of orders."[366] This was certainly a belief that he passed on to his son Douglas. MacArthur's relationship with Taft and the Commission was further damaged by his reserved personality, as he usually refused invitations from the Commission to attend social events or dinner.[367] This refusal to engage in social activities was characteristic of MacArthur but proved a handicap when dealing with politicians who thrive on such occasions to conduct much of their business.

On March 2, 1901, the Spooner Amendment was passed, broadening the legal basis for Presidential appointments in the Philippines. The effect of this act was to provide a legal justification for the status quo, as McKinley had been acting on the basis of such broad authority all along. The very fact that the amendment was passed, however, indicates that MacArthur was correct in his original assessment of the legal basis for presidential action in the Philippines. MacArthur acknowledged that the adoption of the Spooner Amendment reduced his dispute with Taft and the Commission to an academic question.[368] With the passage of this amendment, arrangements were made for a transfer from a military to a civilian government in the Philippines.

---

[366]Bain, p. 80.

[367]Bertoff, p. 201.

[368]Petillo, *Dissertation*, p. 103, see note 85; and Minger, p. 326.

MacArthur's report from the previous year may have been responsible for heightening the determination of the Administration to end military rule in the Islands. Like Taft, they believed the military was responsible for the widespread resistance to American rule.[369] There was a general distrust of the Army on the part of the Administration. With the passage of the Spooner Act, MacArthur was glad to be leaving the Philippines. He viewed the reduction of his authority by the Administration as a humiliation.[370] MacArthur carried this bitterness with him for the rest of his life.

On July 4, 1901, MacArthur turned over command of the Army in the Philippines to General Adna R. Chaffee, who would continue to hold the title of Military Governor.[371] William Howard Taft officially became the Civilian Governor of the Islands. He would now exercise most of the powers formerly held by MacArthur as Military Governor, except in those matters which were clearly of a military nature.[372] After a ceremony formally transferring power to the new civilian government, Taft

---

[369]Leech, p. 572.

[370]Minger, p. 327.

[371]"Ward to Chaffee, 21 June 1901," in *Correspondence*, p. 1286.

[372]see *Correspondence*, p. 1286; and *Five Years of the War Department*, p. 208, for a copy of McKinley's proclamation establishing civilian government in the Philippines.

held a reception for MacArthur at Malacañang Palace, which now became Taft's residence. After the reception, Taft and Chaffee accompanied MacArthur to his ship, the Meade, which sailed first to Nagasaki and then on to San Francisco.[373] MacArthur returned home to the United States amidst little fanfare as the Administration wanted to keep the transfer of power as seemingly peaceful and smooth as possible.[374]

---

[373]*Milwaukee Sentinel*, 5 July 1901.

[374]Miller, p. 175.

Chapter V
Old Soldiers Never Die,
They Just Fade Away

"I still remember the refrain of one of the most popular barrack ballads of that day, which proclaimed, most proudly, that 'Old soldiers never die. They just fade away.' And like the soldier of the ballad, I now close my military career and just fade away."

— Douglas MacArthur[375]

Arthur MacArthur's homecoming did not entirely end his involvement with the Philippines. In April 1902, he was called to testify before the Senate, which held hearings on the American involvement in the Islands. Many Senators viewed MacArthur as the

---

[375]Manchester, p. 661.

most honest witness who had testified before them,[376] despite the fact that his well-developed vocabulary often required some translation. Nevertheless, MacArthur drew criticism from several Senators who felt that he spent too much time expounding the elaborate theories he had developed, instead of merely recounting facts.[377] This was, however, MacArthur's style and not an attempt to cover up or distort the truth. During all of his studies over the years, MacArthur had developed many firm opinions that he believed were relevant to the topics being investigated by the Senate.

Echoing his "Chinese Memorandum and Notes" from two decades earlier, the General testified:

> The United States will soon have to seek trade everywhere on earth, as it must have ever-expanding markets to meet ever-increasing powers of production. In a word, foreign markets will soon become a vital national necessity, a necessity

---

[376]Petillo, p. 55.

[377]Hearings Before the Committee on the Philippines of the United States Senate, National Archives, Record Group 350, Records of the Bureau of Insular Affairs; and Henry F. Graff, ed., *American Imperialism and the Philippine Insurrection: Testimony Taken From Hearings on Affairs in the Philippine Islands before the Senate Committee on the Philippines – 1902* (Boston: Little, Brown and Company, 1969), pp. 141-143. This is an abridged version of the Senate testimony on the Philippines, which includes testimony by Arthur MacArthur.

America cannot dispense with even if she would, and must even fight for if they are not to be secured otherwise...

He went on to add:

The archipelago affords an ideal strategical position. It is the stepping-stone to commanding influence – political, commercial, and military supremacy in the East. It is a base from which American interests can be effectively protected according to such necessities as may arise by process of future evolution.[378]

One of the issues which MacArthur was called upon to testify about concerned the high killed to wounded ratio of Filipino rebels that had been reported by the American Army. MacArthur explained the Filipino strategy to the Senators:

Ordinarily, we should have picked up 1,000 or 1,500 guns on the battlefields around Manila. I doubt if we got ten guns, because of the precious value of those guns to the insurrection and the careful preparation they had made to prevent their falling into our hands. The moment a man was wounded, they

---

[378]Hearings Before the Committee on the Philippines of the United States Senate, National Archives, Record Group 350, Records of the Bureau of Insular Affairs, p. 867.

would seize him and get him off the field, and a man would seize his gun.[379]

MacArthur went on to explain that this strategy was possible because the rebels had "an abundance of men, but a limited number of arms."[380] The effect of this strategy was that the Americans could not get an accurate count of the Filipino wounded because very few of them fell into American hands, and therefore, the statistics compiled by the Army were distorted.

Upon his return to the United States, MacArthur was reunited with Pinky, whom he had not seen for three years. In August 1901, MacArthur stayed at the Auditorium Hotel in Chicago while arrangements were made for a lavish homecoming celebration in his hometown of Milwaukee on September 11. The homecoming banquet was to be sponsored by the Milwaukee Chamber of Commerce, then known as the Milwaukee Merchants and Manufacturers Association. MacArthur's lifelong friend, General Charles King, was put in charge of preparations for the event.[381] All of Milwaukee prepared to greet its

---

[379]*Senate Documents*, No. 331, p. 896.

[380]*Senate Documents*, No. 331, p. 895. The pamphlet about Filipino guerilla warfare tactics translated in Appendix I of MacArthur's report for 1900 in Annual Reports, 1900, supports MacArthur's explanation of this.

[381]Charles King Papers, SHSW; and MacArthur Collection, MCHS both contain information on MacArthur's homecoming.

hero. At the end of the month, MacArthur paid a visit to President McKinley at his home in Canton, Ohio.[382] Several days later, on September 6, President McKinley was shot by anarchist Leon Czolgosz while visiting the Pan American Exposition in Buffalo, New York. The following day, in accordance with MacArthur's wishes, all homecoming plans for MacArthur were abandoned.[383] Initially, it looked as though McKinley might recover, but he died eight days after the shooting.

MacArthur finally made his homecoming to Milwaukee in early October, but on a much smaller scale than initially planned. A banquet was held on MacArthur's behalf by the Commandery of Wisconsin, Loyal Legion of the United States, on October 3, 1901. It was not the large scale public event that had been previously planned to welcome Milwaukee's favorite son. The banquet was only open to members of the Loyal Legion and invited guests.[384] MacArthur was probably more comfortable with this arrangement as he had always

---

[382]"MacArthur to King, 28 August 1901" in Charles King Papers, SHSW.

[383]"MacArthur to King, 8 September 1901," in Charles King Papers, SHSW.

[384]for the proceedings of this banquet, see Captain A. Ross Houston, ed., *War Papers Read Before the Commandery of the State of Wisconsin, Military Order of the Loyal Legion of the United States*, Vol. III (Milwaukee: Burdick and Allen, 1903), pp. 492-524.

tried to avoid large social gatherings whenever possible. MacArthur was much more at home in the company of his old comrades. Later in the month, MacArthur attended the reunion banquet of the 24th Wisconsin.[385] On November 4, 1901, a ceremony was held, sponsored by the Milwaukee Chamber of Commerce, to honor both Generals MacArthur and King. The event was organized by MacArthur's former comrade from the 24th Wisconsin, John Mitchell.[386] MacArthur and King were each presented with a sword from the citizens of Milwaukee in honor of their military service.

Late in 1901, MacArthur was assigned to command the Department of Colorado with its headquarters in Denver. He held this post until March 25, 1902, when he was transferred to command the Department of the Lakes, which included Milwaukee.[387] Shortly after, MacArthur assumed command of the Department of the Lakes, he was called to testify before the Senate about American involvement in the Philippines. MacArthur was next transferred to the Department of the East. Shortly after, he was again transferred, this time to the Department of

---

[385]*Milwaukee Sentinel*, 7 September 1901.

[386]Charles King Papers, SHSW. John Mitchell was the son of Alexander Mitchell, who was active with Arthur's father in Milwaukee's Scottish community.

[387]Carroon, "The Judge and the General," p. 12.

California, which was reorganized as the Division of the Pacific with its headquarters in San Francisco.[388]

MacArthur held a great deal of lingering resentment toward the Army, which he felt had degraded him both during his tenure as Military Governor in the Philippines, by impinging upon his authority, and following his return to the United States, by giving him assignments unworthy of his high rank. MacArthur criticized Secretary of War Elihu Root's plans for the reorganization of the Army along the lines of the German High Command. He also resented that the position of Chief of Staff was filled by junior officers. MacArthur felt that, as ranking officer, he should have been appointed to the post. In 1903, MacArthur publicly predicted a future German-American conflict and criticized the recruitment of German-Americans into the National Guard and the Army. This comment drew a rebuke from President Theodore Roosevelt.[389]

During MacArthur's tenure as commander of the Division of the Pacific, he proposed that an artificial

---

[388]*Milwaukee Sentinel*, 6 September 1912.

[389]Challener, p. 53; and James, p. 40. James says that MacArthur had a bias against Germans stemming from his childhood in German-dominated Milwaukee. There is no evidence to support this hypothesis. It is more likely that MacArthur's strong views on international politics formed the basis for his suspicion of Germans and Germany at this time.

harbor, with military defenses to protect it, be constructed at Los Angeles, then a city of only a few hundred thousand people. MacArthur believed that, with the growing importance of the Pacific region, Los Angeles would become an area of future importance. His proposal was accepted, and the fort constructed to protect the harbor was later named Fort MacArthur in his honor.[390] This plan was consistent with MacArthur's overall view of the increasing importance of the Pacific in world affairs. During his time in command of the Division of the Pacific, MacArthur also was involved in a conflict with San Francisco city officials who felt that he was interfering in civilian affairs when he tried to have saloons bordering the Presidio shut down.[391] This conflict arose out of MacArthur's broad view of the role of the military.

With the outbreak of the Russo-Japanese War in early 1904, MacArthur requested that he be sent to Japan as an observer. While stationed in San Francisco, the General carefully followed reports of the conflict. Always a meticulous student of war, he sent a memorandum to the War Department outlining some of his initial observations of the conflict, along with his request to General Chaffee for assignment to Japan:

---

[390]"Douglas MacArthur to W.W. Hicks, 7 October 1941," in RG-20, MacArthur Archives; and MacArthur, p. 28.

[391]James, pp. 40-41.

It is quite apparent that the Japanese at critical moments have been incapable of the celerity of movement essential to the full achievement of decisive results. Such celerity for example was exemplified by Sheridan in the Appomattox campaign. If, after Liao Yang, Marshall Oyama had moved a column as General Grant moved Sheridan, the Russian Army might possibly have been destroyed, as was the Confederate Army under similar circumstances. That Oyama did not do so, perhaps, arose from the fact that the inflexible organization of his army precluded such rapid movement.

If the foregoing premised are assumed, a conclusion is suggested to the effect that decisive success in war depends quite as much on the organization of an army, in respect of flexibility and celerity of movement, as it does upon minute instruction of officers and men.[392]

The new Secretary of War, William Howard Taft, finally agreed to MacArthur's request in January 1905, reasoning that MacArthur's high rank would allow for closer observation than the Japanese had permitted to the

---

[392]"Memorandum in Respect of the Organization of a Field Army," and "MacArthur to Chaffee," 24 December 1904, in Records of the War Department, National Archives, Record Group 165.

lower ranking officers who were previously dispatched.[393] In connection with this request, MacArthur also asked that, when his assignment with the Japanese Army was complete, he be permitted to make an extensive information gathering tour of Asia. Secretary of War Taft approved MacArthur's trip, probably relieved to do so, because the Administration had no plans to offer MacArthur a position fitting for an officer of his rank.[394]

MacArthur arrived in Tokyo to begin his assignment on March 5, 1905. Four days later, the major battle of the Russo-Japanese War took place at Mukden. MacArthur was unable to reach the front until March 20, eleven days after the Japanese victory at Mukden. On March 24, he wrote to General Chaffee:

> In spite of every possible effort on the part of the Japanese government to expedite my movements to the front, I arrived too late to witness any part of the great battle recently fought in the vicinity, its remote consequences of which are not yet quite apparent here. The defeat of the Russian army was so complete... that it amounts to a disaster.[395]

---

[393]Petillo, Dissertation, p. 128.

[394]Petillo, p. 83.

[395]"MacArthur to Chaffee, 24 March 1905," in Records of the War Department, National Archives, Record Group 165.

Nevertheless, MacArthur stayed on for another next six months observing the Japanese Army in Manchuria and Mongolia. Pinky had accompanied Arthur to Japan, but she remained in Tokyo during this time. On September 10, 1905, MacArthur arrived back in Tokyo, five days after the Treaty of Portsmouth was signed, formally ending the war.[396]

With the war over, MacArthur began to make arrangements for his tour of Asia. On September 17, 1905, MacArthur met with Taft, who was visiting Japan, and made arrangements for his son Douglas to be assigned as his aide during the tour. Taft granted the request, and Douglas arrived in Japan on October 31, 1905. During September and October, MacArthur carefully planned his trip and prepared himself by reading several books about the areas he would visit.[397] This was characteristic of Arthur, who had always studied hard to prepare himself to carry out his duties. MacArthur had originally begun this practice to compensate for his lack of formal military training.

Douglas, now a Lieutenant, joined his father and mother in Japan, and the family began their Asian tour in

---

[396]Petillo, p. 82; and Petillo, Dissertation, p. 134.

[397]Petillo, pp. 84-85. Petillo says that it was probably at Pinky's urging that Arthur made arrangements for Douglas to accompany him on this tour.

early November 1905. This trip would have a lasting
impact on young Douglas. First, the MacArthurs went to
Hong Kong. Next, they visited South China, Singapore,
Java, and Malaya. The MacArthurs then went to Siam,
where they were received by King Chulalongkorn. The
American Envoy in Bangkok reported to Secretary of State,
Elihu Root:

> During the General's stay in this country the
> Siamese Government showed him great respect and
> rendered him every assistance in their power. He
> was given Audience by His Majesty the day
> following his arrival and dined at the Royal Palace a
> week later. His reception by the Crown Prince was
> most cordial and the courtesies shown him by the
> Princes at the head of the several Departments were
> marked.
>
> Indeed outside the reception given His Royal
> Highness Prince Heinrich of Prussia and Prince
> Waldemar of Denmark on their visit to Siam some
> years ago, no man has been accorded such a Royal
> and generous welcome as was the General since I
> have been in this country.[398]

They also spent nearly two months in India during
this trip studying British colonial administration. In
addition, the MacArthurs visited Ceylon and French Indo-

---

[398]"Hamilton King to Elihu Root, 10 April 1906," in Records of the
War Department, National Archives, Record Group 165.

China.[399] In connection with this trip, MacArthur also made a detour to South Africa, which was recovering from the Boer War.[400] It is not surprising that MacArthur made this detour because he had previously expressed an interest in the situation there when he stated, "The Boer is the best individual marksman in the world."[401] In August 1906, MacArthur returned to San Francisco and resumed command of the Division of the Pacific. Douglas went on to enter the Engineer School at Washington Barracks, D.C.[402]

On September 5, 1906, Arthur MacArthur was promoted to the rank of Lieutenant General by a special act of Congress. This made MacArthur only the twelfth man in the history of the United States Army to hold this rank, the highest in the Army up to that time. The rank was to be abolished with MacArthur's retirement, but it was later revived during World War I.[403] The promotion did

---

[399]James, p. 41; and MacArthur, pp. 30-31; and Petillo, Dissertation, p. 134. See also, Petillo, pp. 85-95.

[400]Charles King Pagers, SHSW; and Carroon, "The Judge and the General," p. 12; and *Milwaukee Sentinel*, 6 September 1912.

[401]*Senate Documents*, No. 331, p. 897.

[402]James, p. 41.

[403]Usher, p. 1847; and Cartoon, "The Judge and the General," p. 12; and Manchester, p. 37; and Milwaukee Sent Petillo, Dissertation, p. 146; and Lee and Henschel, p. 23; and Carroon, "The Judge and

nothing to relieve the bitterness MacArthur felt toward the Army. The new Army was leaving old soldiers like MacArthur behind. Even though he was the highest ranking officer in the Army, MacArthur was not named Chief of Staff. His lack of West Point training and his conflict with the political authorities, especially Secretary of War William Howard Taft, combined to deny him the position warranted by his rank.[404] As a result, MacArthur became more and more isolated from the Army he had devoted his life to.

At the beginning of 1907, MacArthur was informed that the administrative units known as Divisions would be abolished. He was offered command of the Eastern Department, a further reduction in his responsibilities, but he declined to accept it. MacArthur's bitterness toward the new Army was reflected in a letter he wrote to Secretary of War Taft early in 1907:

> The office of Lieutenant General which I now hold, was originally intended to subserve only the highest purposes of military expediency... it is now so much depressed, that in effect it has become merely a title.

---

the General," p. 12. Minger, p. 211 incorrectly claims that Taft recommended MacArthur for Chief of Staff on two occasions.

[404]Petillo, Dissertation, p. 146; and Lee and Henschel, p. 23; and Carroon, "The Judge and the General," p. 12. Minger, p. 211.

MacArthur's Oath of Office upon accepting
his promotion to the rank of Lieutenant General

By process of current events it has been medicized, and divested of prestige, dignity, and influence.[405]

MacArthur requested that he be sent to Milwaukee, where he would be available for such special assignments as the War Department might designate and where he could prepare a report on his Asian tour.[406] MacArthur wrote, "the sooner the depressing condition is terminated, the better it will be for all the interests involved."[407] Taft granted MacArthur's request and he returned to his hometown on May 20, 1907.[408]

Milwaukee had always given MacArthur a sense of security. His boyhood friends and former comrades of the 24th Wisconsin were there, and he always seemed to feel most comfortable in their company. At a time when the Army had turned its back on him, MacArthur knew he could return to Milwaukee and always find a home. The importance of Milwaukee to MacArthur was evident when he reflected:

> I have had some pleasant occasions in my life, as I have gone from one thing to another; but nothing gives me so much pleasure and satisfaction as returning here to Milwaukee and being greeted by

---

[405]Petillo, p. 94.

[406]James, p. 42.

[407]Petillo, p. 94.

[408]*Milwaukee Sentinel*, 6 September 1912.

fifty men whom I knew here as boys in the early days.... It is a fortunate thing when a man is bred into a community in such a way that he returns thereto, after many years' absence, with a consciousness and absolute certainty that he will find his boyish associates.... I fit in completely and comfortably, as though I had never been away.[409]

The group security that had been an important factor throughout Arthur's life, he once again found in his hometown.

Although he was more isolated than ever from the Army, MacArthur continued to speak out on Asian affairs, emphasizing their importance to American strategic interests. In a speech to the annual convention of the Wisconsin Banker's Association in 1907, MacArthur again put forth his view that the proper role for the United States in the Philippines was to prepare the Filipinos for self-government:

Fortunately the word "colony" has, as yet, no place in the lexicon of American political administration...

On this auspicious occasion, as a first contribution, I venture to suggest that the Philippine Archipelago be described as "Tuitionary Territory," ad for convenient reference shall be known as "a Tuitionate," that is to say, a territory the inhabitants

---

[409]*MacArthurs of Milwaukee*, pp. 20-21.

of which are being tutored in the art of self-government, with a view to such final disposition as the progress of events may suggest; and also, with the distinct understanding that while independence is clearly within the scope of probability, incorporation into the continental part of the republic is absolutely precluded for all time.[410]

In a speech to the Old Settler's Club in Milwaukee, on February 22, 1908, MacArthur stated that "Japan must be regarded as master of the ocean."[411] While ruling out a Japanese-American conflict in the near future, MacArthur predicted that such a conflict could develop.[412] History would prove him correct in his assessment of the situation. In July 1908, the Wisconsin State Bar Association proposed that Arthur MacArthur be Wisconsin's candidate for the Republican presidential nomination.[413] MacArthur apparently had no desire to challenge his old nemesis, William Howard Taft, and he politely declined to enter the political arena.

---

[410]Speech to Wisconsin Banker's Association, pp. 163-164, in Records of the War Department, National Archives, Record Group 165.

[411]Challener, p. 231.

[412]Ibid.; and Manchester, p. 37.

[413]Carroon, "The Judge and the General," p. 13.

On June 2, 1909, after forty-seven years of military service, Arthur MacArthur retired from the Army at the mandatory retirement age of sixty-four. He did so quietly and without ceremony.[414] MacArthur felt that the Army had abandoned and humiliated him, so he quietly faded away into retirement. On the day of his retirement, MacArthur told a reporter:

> There is no reason for any special ceremony, the day
> is of deep significance to me, of course, but an army
> officer's retirement is never a ceremonious event. I
> am no longer in active service, but my deep interest
> in military affairs, I am sure, will never cease.[415]

After returning to Milwaukee, the MacArthurs made their home at 575 (now 1101) Marshall Street. Arthur became an active member of the Milwaukee community as his father had been many years before. Arthur was involved with the St. Andrew's Society and spoke at the dedication of a monument to the Scottish poet Robert Burns in Milwaukee on June 26, 1909.[416] Governor James Davidson appointed him to serve on the State Commission planning the celebration of the victory of Commodore

---

[414]Special Order 126, War Department, 2 June 1909 in MacArthur Correspondence, National Archives.

[415]*Milwaukee Sentinel*, 2 June 1909 and 6 September 1912.

[416]*The Evening Wisconsin*, 26 June 1909; and Carroon, "The Judge and the General," p. 13.

Oliver Hazzard Perry at Putin Bay during the War of 1812.[417] Arthur also served as President of the Loyal Legion of the United States, a veterans group composed mainly of Civil War veterans.[418] He was also an active member of the Grand Army of the Republic, Walcott Post, in Milwaukee.[419]

Macarthur organized a reunion of the 24th Wisconsin, which was held in Milwaukee on November 27, 1909. He strove for it to be an impressive event, as he predicted it could be the last such reunion of his old Civil War regiment. MacArthur wrote to former Milwaukee Congressman Theobald Otjen:

> As it will probably be the last formal meeting of the regiment, I am very much interested in making the event as impressive as possible.
>
> As the regiment was largely recruited within the limits of the district you represented so long in Congress, it would be appropriate if you could make it convenient to attend what may be the last ceremonial in its history.
>
> I therefore take great pleasure in extending a cordial invitation to be present with us on this interesting

---

[417]*The Evening Wisconsin*, 26 June 1909.

[418]James, p. 42; and Cartoon, "The Judge and the General." p. 13; and Charles King Papers, SHSW.

[419]Carroon, "The Judge and the General," p. 13.

occasion; and would regard it as a personal favor if you can possibly arrange to that end.[420]

It would not be the last reunion, but it was an unforgettable event.

MacArthur took great care in arranging the event because he looked back fondly to his early days in the Army and felt a special attachment to the men who had served with him in the 24th Wisconsin. The new Army had turned its back on MacArthur, but memories of the past were alive for him to fill the void.

During his years of retirement, MacArthur suffered from a severe case of hyperacidity of the stomach.[421] This condition may very well have been aggravated by the bitterness which had built up in him since his days in the Philippines, but which his austere nature did not allow him to express outwardly. In 1910, MacArthur was suggested as a possible gubernatorial candidate, but again declined to enter politics.[422] Like his father before him, he retired to his library and continued his studies. He took a particular interest in political history and also studied the classics. MacArthur's social life, outside of his civic activities, was confined mainly to regular gatherings with

---

[420]"MacArthur to Otjen, 16 November 1909," in MacArthur Collection, MCHS.

[421]James, p. 42.

[422]Carroon, *The Judge and the General*, p. 13.

a small group of his old boyhood friends, including Charles King and James Flanders.[423]

On September 5, 1912, the Milwaukee Chamber of Commerce sponsored a reunion banquet for the surviving members of the 24th Wisconsin regiment that it had helped to raise fifty years earlier. The date chosen for the reunion was exactly fifty years to the day since the regiment left Milwaukee on the train bound for the front. Ninety survivors of the regiment were present for the occasion. King recounted:

> For over a year, the General had suffered from hyperacidity of the stomach. Of late, his condition had aroused the anxiety of Mrs. MacArthur, and of their near neighbor, myself. The day had been the hottest of the season. The General had taken little nourishment for three days previous, and, fearing the result, Mrs. MacArthur begged him not to go, but aided him to dress when she found he could not be dissuaded.[424]

The fact that Arthur insisted on attending the banquet despite his ill-health reflects the deep attachment he had to his old regiment. E.B. Parsons presided at the banquet, and, after some opening remarks, he called upon his old

---

[423]*Milwaukee Journal*, 6 September 1912.

[424]"King to Adjutant General, 7 September 1912," in Charles King Papers, SHSW; *Milwaukee Sentinel*, 6 September 1912.

friend and commander Arthur to address the men of the regiment. Their Colonel rose and began to speak:

> Comrades, such occasions as these are appreciated only when they are over. We tonight can never realize what enjoyment the reminiscences of this meeting will bring. Little did we imagine fifty years ago, that we should ever be allowed to gather in this way. Little did we think on that march to Atlanta that so many of us would be spared to see Wisconsin again. Your indomitable regiment...,

MacArthur paused, "Comrades, I am too weak to proceed." He then slumped to his chair, and his head fell forward. He died almost instantly, the victim of an apoplectic stroke.[425] The *Milwaukee Sentinel* reported the scene in the room where MacArthur had died:

> One by one, the old soldiers turned away. They drew handkerchiefs from their pockets and wiped their eyes. Then one by one, they knelt by the side of their stricken commander in reverent attitude.

> 'Our father. which art in heaven,' began one of the veterans. As the words left his lips the others joined in, a somber gathering transformed from one of merry making but a few minutes before.

> At the conclusion of the prayer, as the soldiers arose, one of them took down one of the American flags

---

[425]*Milwaukee Sentinel*, 6 September 1912.

that had adorned the walls and spread the stars and stripes over the dead commander. Silently the soldiers left the hall. The reunion was ended.[426]

MacArthur died where he had often expressed a wish to die, in the midst of his men. E.B. Parsons, who had presided at the banquet, was overcome with shock at the death of his long-time friend and suffered a stroke of paralysis. He died two weeks later. Arthur's lifelong friend Charles King went personally to the MacArthur home on Marshall Street to break the tragic news to Mrs. MacArthur. Upon hearing the news of her husband's death, Pinky collapsed and had to be attended to by a physician.[427]

MacArthur's body was taken to the undertaker and then to the family home on Marshall Street. General King sent telegrams to Arthur's two sons, Arthur III, who was then at the Naval College in Newport, Rhode Island, and Douglas, who was then at Fort Leavenworth, informing them of their father's death. At Pinky's request, General King handled the arrangements for the funeral of his close friend. In accordance with MacArthur's expressed wishes, the funeral was conducted with the utmost simplicity and

---

[426]Ibid.

[427]Ibid.

with no military honors.[428] MacArthur's bitterness toward the Army, which he felt had abandoned him, caused him to make these specific directions long before his death.

Charles King reported details of the funeral to the Adjutant General in a letter dated September 10, 1912:

On Monday morning, September 9th, the funeral service was held at the family residence, 575 Marshall Street, attended by veterans of the 24th Wisconsin Vol. Infantry, and of the Military Order of the Loyal Legion. Colonel John L. Glen was the only officer of the active list, except the General's sons, to attend from either Army or Navy. Military display of every kind having been forbidden by the family, as enjoined by the General in recent years. The remains were clothed in civilian dress, and the flag alone was placed upon the casket and buried with him.

An hour later, the internment took place in the MacArthur lot at Forest Home Cemetery. Only the family, the bearers, and a few old and intimate friends accompanied the body to this point, where the committal was read by the officiating clergyman and "Light's Out" sounded by the trumpeter of the

---

[428]Ibid., and "King to Adjutant General, 7 September 1912," in Charles King Papers, SHSW.

Loyal Legion of which General MacArthur was in chief command.[429]

Among the honorary pallbearers at the funeral were Charles King, James G. Flanders, Governor Francis McGovern, and former Governor George Peck.[430] Years later, Douglas MacArthur arranged for his father's body to be transferred for burial in Arlington National Cemetery.[431]

The entire city mourned MacArthur's death, and the Mayor of Milwaukee, G.A. Bading, issued a proclamation ordering flags in city to be flown at half-mast:

Our whole nation today mourns the sudden and untimely death of Lieutenant General Arthur MacArthur.

The nation's greatest soldier, Wisconsin's most famous military son, Milwaukee's brilliant offering in the time of the Civil War, his life and deeds have been our pride.

Such honor as was his has come to few men in America, and certainly to none other in Wisconsin

---

[429]"King to Adjutant General, 10 September 1912," in "Lt. Gen. A. MacArthur, Correspondence and Records, War Department, 1862-1944, National Archives, Microcopy 1604, Roll 277.

[430]*Milwaukee Sentinel*, 10 September 1912.

[431]Carroon, "The Judge and the General," p 1.

or Milwaukee. Let us do what we can to immortalize his memory.[432]

The final chapter on the life of Arthur MacArthur was closed. Perhaps years later, when Douglas MacArthur quoted the old West Point barracks ballad that declared, "Old soldiers never die, they just fade away," his thoughts drifted back to his father. Arthur MacArthur had indeed faded away, abandoned by the Army to which he had dedicated his life.

---

[432]*Milwaukee Journal,* 6 September 1912.

Conclusion

S hortly after the death of Arthur MacArthur, Charles King received a letter from Mr. E.R. Kennedy, an old schoolmate of his and MacArthur's, who was also a relative of the Editors of the Houghton Mifflin Company:

My dear Charley:

At the time we gave MacArthur the schoolmates' welcome home I heard something indefinite about his being engaged in writing what was intended to be a monumental work - the result of his observations of the war between Russia and Japan. What is there to be said about that; and did Arthur leave anything like an autobiography or recollections? If so and they were incomplete, you, it seems to me, are the only man fitted to complete them. If there is nothing of his to take the place of it a regular biography in your charming style would, I feel sure, make a successful book, would fix the record of his life permanently in literature, and would afford you, his schoolmate and playmate and lifetime friend, that solemn pride and satisfaction which you so touchingly referred to as my feeling over having done something for the memory of General Baker.[433]

Unfortunately, for unknown reasons, King never undertook the project, though he was a prolific writer and had published several works, including a biography of General Grant. Perhaps, King could not bring himself to write about his lifelong friend because it was a subject too close to himself. King did leave some small, unpublished recollections of MacArthur, but most of these were written before the death of his friend.

Arthur MacArthur has since been neglected by historians and his life has never received the attention it deserves. Many books dealing with the American involvement in the Philippines fail even to mention his name. Yet, to properly understand the development of American policy in the Philippine Islands and the suppression of the insurrection, it is imperative that Arthur MacArthur be studied. Most of the studies of MacArthur's life have been done in connection with the study of Douglas MacArthur, whose career parallels his father's in many ways. The best work done in this regard has been by Carol Morris Petillo and D. Clayton James. The

---

[433]"Kennedy to King, 12 September 1912." in *Charles King Papers*, SHSW.

exception to this was Kenneth Ray Young's comprehensive scholarly biography, *The General's General*, but in the quarter-century since its publication, Arthur MacArthur is still not accorded the attention he deserves in American history books. This is in part due to a paucity of personal records. While a great deal of official records documenting his career are available to researchers, the General's personal papers, which were in the possession of his son Douglas, were destroyed in the Philippines during World War II.

Despite the paucity of scholarly work on his life and career, Arthur MacArthur was not totally forgotten. On September 7, 1942, a monument was dedicated to Arthur MacArthur in Chicopee Falls, Massachusetts, where he was born. The monument was erected in a square near the house where he had been born. The square was named MacArthur Square in his honor. Efforts to preserve the home where MacArthur was born as a historical landmark failed, and it was subsequently destroyed.[434] Arthur's success in the military was extended through the careers of his sons. The career of Douglas MacArthur is well known. Arthur's eldest son, Arthur III, went on to achieve the rank of Captain in the Navy. He received the Navy Cross and the Distinguished Service Medal for his service

---

[434]MacArthur Collections. MCHS.

in World War I. Sadly, his distinguished career was cut short when Arthur III died of appendicitis on December 2, 1923. He was buried near his father at Arlington National Cemetery.[435]

The study of the life of Arthur MacArthur sheds light on the period of American history from the Civil War through the 1800s and into the twentieth century as America became a world power. He is a representative figure of his time. Indeed, MacArthur was one of the last of the self-taught American military leaders. He studied harder than any officer in the service and displayed great foresight. He understood the growing importance of the Pacific Theatre to American strategic interests long before his assignment to the Philippines. MacArthur also played a key role in bringing the Army into the twentieth century through his reform efforts during his time in the Adjutant General's office, as well as during his tenure as Military Governor in the Philippines. He also guided the careers of many of the next generation of American military leaders, including Peyton March, Black Jack Pershing, Frederick Funston, and others. Many of these men would also be instrumental in advancing the military career of his son Douglas. Despite his remarkable achievements, the new Army, which emerged at the turn of the century, had no place for the old General, and it left him behind.

---

[435]MacArthur, p 17.

This book has merely been a survey of the life of this great individual in the hope that it will help bring the life and career of this great American to the attention of a new generation. The motto of West Point, 'Duty, Honor, Country,' seems an appropriate epitaph for Arthur MacArthur, even though he never attended the prestigious military institution. As much as anyone, Arthur MacArthur embodied these noble words.

The Spelling of Macarthur

A subject that has been the object of some speculation in MacArthur scholarship is the changing of the spelling of the family name from McArthur to MacArthur. When and why this change occurred is unclear, but it is necessary to attempt to shed some light on the matter.

Among the various attempts to answer this question, one scholar erroneously suggested that it was Douglas MacArthur who instigated the change in the spelling of the family name.[436] D. Clayton James simply states that it is not known when the spelling was changed [437] and does not suggest an answer. Another source claims that Arthur MacArthur Jr. began using the spelling MacArthur beginning with his military career in 1862, and that Judge

---

[436]Robert W. Wells, *Yesterday's Milwaukee* (E.A. Seemann Publishing Inc., Miami, 1976) p 29.

[437]James, p. 638.

MacArthur later adopted this spelling for the sake of consistency.[438] None of these answers are correct.

Civil War records, and letters written by MacArthur during the War, clearly indicate that Arthur Jr. continued to use the spelling McArthur throughout the war.[439] Judge MacArthur used the spelling McArthur throughout the Civil War also, as is indicated in his correspondence with his friend Charles D. Robinson.[440] It is clear that this change did not occur until after the Civil War. Judge MacArthur continued to use the spelling throughout his tenure as Circuit Court Judge in Milwaukee as indicated by court records.[441] Published works reveal that Judge MacArthur had adopted the spelling MacArthur by the late 1870s. Douglas, who was born in 1880, could not have instituted the change as both Arthur Jr. and his father were using the new spelling consistently before his birth. The spelling change was probably adopted by the family early in the 1870s.

The reasons for the spelling change are even less clear. It has been speculated that the reason for the change was that Arthur Jr. was the victim of a military clerk who spelled it, MacArthur, at the beginning of his military

---

[438]*MacArthurs of Milwaukee*, p. 49.

[439]*Roster of Wisconsin Volunteers*, p. 56.

[440]Robinson Papers, SHSW.

[441]James, p 638, and *MacArthurs of Milwaukee*, p. 49.

career in 1862.[442] This is not true, as indicated by Civil War records. A military clerk would be more likely to delete a letter than to add one. If this were the case, it would be unlikely that Judge MacArthur would change the spelling of his name merely for consistency.

Another hypothesis is that Arthur, Jr. changed the spelling to MacArthur because he felt it was more Scottish.[443] This is a plausible reason for the change, but it is far more likely that Judge MacArthur, who took great pride in his Scottish heritage, would be responsible for the change. The change in the spelling of the family name was taken quite seriously by Judge MacArthur; Arthur Sr. made a special point of correcting a correspondent, in a letter dated 10 June 1887, that the proper spelling of the family name was MacArthur and not McArthur.[444] This seems to suggest that Judge MacArthur played an important role in changing the spelling.

It seems that Judge MacArthur changed the spelling of the family name to MacArthur because it was more Scottish. He probably did so when he moved to Washington, D.C., to accept his appointment on the

---

[442]*MacArthurs of Milwaukee*, p 49.

[443]Ibid.

[444]"Arthur MacArthur to Ben W. Austine, 10 June 1887," in RG-2O, MacArthur Archives.

Supreme Court of the District of Columbia. It would be convenient to make such a change when he established himself in a new city. Arthur Jr. was probably consulted by his father on the matter and he changed the spelling of his name also around this time.

Army Record of Lieutenant General MacArthur

(Born June 2, 1845, Springfield, Mass.)*

WAR OF THE REBELLION, 1861-65

First lieutenant and adjutant, Twenty-fourth Wisconsin infantry, August 4, 1862. Major, January 25, 1864. Lieutenant colonel, May 3, 1865. Brevet lieutenant colonel, March 13, 1865, for "gallant and meritorious services in the battles of Perryville, Ky., Stone River, Missionary Ridge and Dandridge, Tenn." Brevet colonel, March 13, 1865, for "gallant and meritorious services in the battle of Franklin, Tenn., and in the Atlanta campaign." Commissioned colonel, Twenty-fourth Wisconsin infantry, June 13, 1865, but not mustered — his regiment

---

*As published by the Military Order of the Loyal Legion of the United States, Headquarters Commandery of the State of Wisconsin. Circular No. 12, Series 1912, Whole No. 506, October 12, 1912.

having been depleted by the casualties of battle to less than the minimum strength.

Medal of honor "for coolness and conspicuous bravery in action in seizing the colors of his regiment at a critical moment and planting them on the captured works on the crest of Missionary Ridge, Tenn., November 25, 1863, while serving as first lieutenant and adjutant, Twenty-fourth Wisconsin infantry."

BATTLES AND ENGAGEMENTS

Perryville, Stone River, Dandridge, Missionary Ridge, Resaca, Adairsville, New Hope Church, Kenesaw Mountain, Peach Tree Creek, Jonesboro, Lovejoy's Station, Atlanta, Franklin.

Wounded right wrist and right breast at Kenesaw, but refused to leave the field. Severely wounded left breast, right shoulder, and left leg at Franklin.

Honorably mustered out, June 10, 1865.

REGULAR SERVICE, 1866-1009

Second lieutenant, Seventeenth infantry, February 23, 1866; first lieutenant, Seventeenth infantry, February 23, 1866. Captain, Thirty-sixth infantry, July 28, 1866 — and Thirteenth infantry, 1870, on consolidation. Major and assistant adjutant general, July 1, 1889. Lieutenant colonel

and assistant adjutant general, May 26, 1896. Brigadier
general, January 2, 1900. Major general, February 5, 1901.
Lieutenant general, September 15, 1906; retired June 2,
1909.

SPANISH AND FILIPINO WARS, 1898-1901

Brigadier general, U.S. Volunteers, May 27, 1898.
Major general, August 13, 1898. Commanding First
brigade, Independent Division, Eighth Army Corps, Camp
Merritt, San Francisco, June 12, 1898, and third expedition
to Manila, June-July, 1898. Commanding First brigade,
First division, Eighth Army Corps in advance on Manila,
July-August, and at battle of Manila, August 13, 1898.
Commanding Second division, Eighth Army Corps,
Manila, August, 1898, to February, 1899. Repulse of
insurgent attack north and east front, Manila, February 4-
5, 1899. Advance on Caloocan. Battle of Caloocan,
February 10.

Commanding the advance upon the successive
capitals of the insurgent government — Malolos, San
Fernando and Tarlac — and in the battles of Tuliajon, Polo,
Marilao, Bigaa, Guiguinto (Malolos occupied March 31,
1899) — passage of the Bagbag and of the Rio Grande;
battles of Santo Tomas (San Fernando occupied May 6),
Bacolor, Calulit, Angeles (Tarlac occupied May 12),

capture of Banban and in the general engagement of San Fernando, June 16.

Commanding department of Northern Luzon, April 1, 1899, to May 5, 1900.

Commanding division of the Philippines and military governor of the Philippine islands, May 5, 1900, to July 4, 1901.

Sent to seat of war between Russia and Japan as an observer; also to South Africa and other parts of the world.

(Died, September 5, 1912, Milwaukee, Wisconsin)

Appendix III

In Memoriam

Companion Arthur Macarthur*

In twenty commonwealths of our united Nation, and in twenty-one commanderies of the Loyal Legion, surviving veterans of our greatest war are assembled, as so wisely ordered and so well said in the initial circular of its new commander-in-chief, "in tender memory" of him whose name so recently stood foremost on its rolls. Lieutenant general in the Army and chief in command of the Loyal Legion, he was doubly ours, for it was here, within the limits of this very city — the home of his boyhood and of his later years, — within the compass of these very walls — the home of the soldier associations of his soldierly life, — and within the span of a single month

---

*As published by the Military Order of the Loyal Legion of the United States, Headquarters Commandery of the State of Wisconsin. Circular No. 12, Series 1912, Whole No. 506, October 12, 1912.

that he was borne from our midst across the threshold of Immortality.

Thrice in succession he had been our commander. Longer still we fondly hoped to hail him our commander-in-chief; but longer yet by far he had been our companion, our comrade and our friend. The loss which falls so heavily upon the Military Order of the Loyal Legion of the United States falls most heavily upon the Commandery of the State of Wisconsin — upon us who for more than half a century have best known, and who now most sorely miss him.

The bare facts of the official record, published herewith, are sufficient to place the name of Arthur MacArthur among those of the Nation's greatest leaders, and to proclaim him the foremost among the soldiers of our state. But beyond these facts there lives a story of struggle and achievement — of self-discipline and self-education — little known and seldom equaled.

Appointed to the adjutancy of the Twenty-fourth Wisconsin Infantry, his first appearance on parade aroused little less than derision which had barely abated when, one month later, the regiment received its fiery baptism in front of Chaplin Hills, where a new light fell upon its boy adjutant. Three months more and it was his voice that steadied the ranks in the fierce grapple at Stone's River. Another year and at Missionary Ridge they breasted the heights at the heels of the lad at whom the year before they laughed. Not yet nineteen, yet major commanding, he led them on the Tennessee, cheered them at Dandridge and later at Resaca, held them at Kenesaw against the mad whirl of a stricken brigade, stormed with them the lines of Atlanta and, last of his early battles, splendidly handled them in the bloody fight at Franklin until, thrice wounded, he was borne from the field. It was their "boy colonel," eulogized by corps and division commanders, that marched them home to final muster out. It was their boy colonel that lived from that time forth the hero of the Milwaukee regiment.

Then followed the long years in the regular service — years of thought, and study and wide reading that led to his selection from all the captains the line for promotion to the staff, and later to high command fur the second time in the volunteers. It came with the Spanish War quickly followed by the voyage to Manila, and the fall of the flag of Spain, which doubled in a day the stars upon MacArthur's shoulders. Then came the long and arduous campaign consequent upon the revolt Aguinaldo, with its reward of a generalship in the permanent establishment. Then, greatest command and greatest opportunity of all, the governor generalship of the Philippine Islands. Later followed the tours of observation in Asia and South Africa, the return to the old home and old friends bearing the highest rank in our military service; latest of all, the last night on earth, facing and addressing the very men whom he had led in battle after battle fifty years ago. From the command of those men he had been graduated into the life career in the regular army. From the midst of those men, with whom he had dared death on field after field, he passed onward to the life eternal.

Within the limits of official tribute it is impossible to detail the achievements of our honored commander. Years of profound study had raised him in scholarship and statesmanship to a plane even with that of his brilliant soldiership. There was no office in the gift of the American people which he was not amply fitted to adorn. The Army looked upon him as by far its ablest general; the people hardly knew him for he shrank instinctively from ostentation. It is among us — Companions of the Legion, with whom in his last years he chiefly associated — that his powers were preeminently shown. The addresses delivered since his homecoming stand unexcelled in depth, in thought and wisdom. The inspiration of his presence and leadership lent to our ceremonies new grace and dignity. The example of his fervent patriotism, his unshaken loyalty, his silent and soldierly acceptance of conditions little looked for in view of his great services and exalted rank, and with it all the glow of his attachment to old comradeships and old associations, had served to rouse responsive chords in every heart, and to make the boy comrade of our school days, the boy colonel of the war days, the accomplished soldier scholar of the national army — last of its illustrious line of lieutenant generals — an idol in the eyes of the survivors of his old regiment, and the most honored and revered companion of our knightly Order.

In silent submission, like unto his own, we bow before the mandate of Omnipotence. In soldier mourning we drape the colors he had ever loved and glorified. In sympathy unspeakable we pay our humble tribute before the devoted wife, and the gallant sons who were his hope and pride. Wisconsin received again her unrivaled General when from our arms the flag-draped form returned to earth, and the trumpets of the Loyal Legion — the only martial honors he would permit — sang "Lights Out" over our great commander's grave.

CHARLES KING,

F. C. WINKLER,

THOMAS E. BALDING,

Committee

Bibliography

Primary Sources

Address of Arthur McArthur Esq. on the 4th Anniversary of the Right Worthy Grand Lodge of Wisconsin. Milwaukee: Sentinel and Gazette Steam Press Print, 1850.

Affairs in the Philippine Islands, Hearings Before the Committee on the Philippines of the United States Senate. 57th Congress, 1st Session. Document No. 331, Part 2. Washington: U.S. Government Printing Office, 1902.

Annual Reports of the War Department for the Fiscal Year Ended June 30, 1899: Report of the Major General Commanding the Army. Part 2. Washington: U.S. Government Printing Office, 1899.

Annual Reports of the War Department for the Fiscal Year Ended June 30, 1900: Report of the Lieutenant General Commanding the Army. Part 3. Washington: U.S. Government Printing Office, 1900.

Annual Reports of the War Department for the Fiscal Year Ended June 30, 1900: Report of the Military Governor of the Philippine Islands on Civil Affairs. Washington: U.S. Government Printing Office, 1900.

The Centennial Anniversary of the Birthday of Robert Burns as Commemorated by his Countrymen in the City of Milwaukee, Wisconsin, January 25, 1859. Milwaukee: Daily News Book and Job Steam Printing Establishment, 1859.

Charles King Collection. Milwaukee County Historical Society.

Charles King Papers. Micro 479. State Historical Society of Wisconsin.

Charles D. Robinson Papers. SC 229. State Historical Society of Wisconsin.

Correspondence Relating to the War with Spain. Washington: U.S. Government Printing Office, 1902.

Dewey, George. *Autobiography of George Dewey, Admiral of the Navy.* New York: Charles Scribner's Sons, 1913.

Diary of Brigadier General Charles King During the Philippine Insurrection. Wis. Mss. KW (Micro 257). State Historical Society of Wisconsin.

The Evening Wisconsin, 27 August 1896.

The Evening Wisconsin, 26 June 1901.

The Evening Wisconsin, 7 September 1912.

Five Years of the War Department Following the War with Spain, 1899-1903, As Shown in the Annual Reports of the Secretary of War. Washington: U.S. Government Printing Office, 1904.

Funston, Frederick. *Memories of Two Wars: Cuban and Philippine Experiences.* New York: Charles Scribner's Sons, 1911.

General William Mitchell Correspondence, 1888, 1893-1904, 1927. (Restricted). Micro 293. State Historical Society of Wisconsin.

Graff, Henry F., Ed. *American Imperialism and the Philippine Insurrection: Testimony taken from the Hearings on Affairs in the Philippine Islands before the Senate Committee on the Philippines – 1902.* Boston: Little, Brown and Company, 1969.

Houston, Captain A. Ross, Ed. *War Papers Read Before the Commandery of the State of Wisconsin, Military Order of the Loyal Legion of the United States, Vol. I.* Milwaukee: Burdick, Armitage and Allen, 1891.

Houston, Captain A. Ross, Ed. *War Papers Read Before the Commandery of the State of Wisconsin, Military Order of the Loyal Legion of the United States, Vol. III.* Milwaukee: Burdick and Allen, 1903.

"Lt. Gen. A. MacArthur, Correspondence and Records, War Department, 1862-1944, National Archives, Microcopy 1604, Roll 277.

MacArthur, Douglas. *Reminiscences*. New York: McGraw Hill Book Company, 1964.

MacArthur Collection. Milwaukee County Historical Society.

Military Order of the Loyal Legion of the United States, Commandery of the State of Wisconsin, 1909-1914, Circulars No. 447-545.

Milwaukee Journal, 9 September 1901.

Milwaukee Journal, 6 September 1912.

Milwaukee Sentinel, 11 August 1862.

Milwaukee Sentinel, 15 August 1862.

Milwaukee Sentinel, 15 June 1865.

Milwaukee Sentinel, 16 June 1865.

Milwaukee Sentinel, 5 July 1901.

Milwaukee Sentinel, 7 September 1901.

Milwaukee Sentinel, 9 September 1901.

Milwaukee Sentinel, 2 June 1909.

Milwaukee Sentinel, 6 September 1912.

Milwaukee Sentinel, 9 September 1912.

Milwaukee Sentinel, 10 September 1912.

National Archives. Lt. Gen. A. MacArthur, Correspondence and Records, War Department, 1862-1944, Microcopy 1064, Roll 277.

National Archives, Record Group 165, Records of the War Department.

National Archives, Record Group 350, Bureau of Insular Affairs.

Papers of Lieutenant General Arthur MacArthur. RG-20. MacArthur Memorial Archives.

Roster of Wisconsin Volunteers, War of the Rebellion 1861-1865, Vol. II. Madison: Democrat Printing Co.-State Printers, 1886.

St. Andrew's Collection. Milwaukee County Historical Society.

Trobriand, Philippe Regis de, *Army Life in Dakota*. Chicago: Lakeview Press, 1941.

Wisconsin Necrology. State Historical Society of Wisconsin.

Wisconsin Volunteers, War of the Rebellion, 1861-1865. Madison: State of Wisconsin-Democrat Printing Company, 1914.

Secondary Sources

"Arthur MacArthur," pp. 95-96 in *Outlook*, September 21, 1912.

Bain, David Havard. *Sitting in Darkness; Americans in the Philippines*. Boston: Houghton Mifflin Co., 1984.

Beisner, Robert L. *From the Old Diplomacy to the New, 1865-1900*. Arlington Heights, IL: Harlan Davidson, Inc., 1975.

Bertoff, Rowland Tappan. "Taft and MacArthur, 1900: A Study in Civil-Military Relations," pp. 196-213 in *World Politics: A Quarterly Journal of International Relations*, 5 (1953).

Blair, Clay Jr. *MacArthur*. New York: Pocket Books, 1977.

Boller, Paul F. *Presidential Campaigns*. New York: Oxford University Press, 1984.

Braisted, William Reynolds. *The United States Navy in the Pacific, 1897-1909*. New York: Greenwood Press, Publishers, 1969.

Carroon, Robert G. "Scotsmen in Old Milwaukee," pp. 20-33 in *Historical Messenger of the Milwaukee County Historical Center*, 25 (March, 1969)

Challener, Richard D. *Admirals, Generals, and American Foreign Policy 1898-1914*. Princeton: Princeton University Press, 1973.

Conzen, Kathleen Neils. *Immigrant Milwaukee. 1836-1860: Accommodation and Community in a Frontier City*. Cambridge: Harvard University Press, 1976.

Cosmas, Graham A. *An Army for Empire; The United States Army in the Spanish-American War*. Columbia, MO: University of Missouri Press, 1971.

Current, Richard N. *The History of Wisconsin II: The Civil War Era, 1848-1873*. Madison: State Historical Society of Wisconsin, 1976.

Dictionary of Wisconsin Biography. Madison: State Historical Society of Wisconsin, 1960.

Draper, Lyman Copeland, Ed. *Collections of the State Historical Society of Wisconsin, Vol. VI.* Madison: State Historical Society of Wisconsin, 1908.

Elliott, Charles Burke. *The Philippines: To the End of the Commission Government: A Study in Tropical Democracy.* Indianapolis: The Bobbs-Merrill Company Publishers, 1917.

Elliott, Charles Burke. *The Philippines: To the End of the Military Regime.* Indianapolis: The Bobbs-Merrill Company Publishers, 1916.

Estabrook, Charles E., Ed. *Records and Sketches of Military Organizations.* Madison: State of Wisconsin-Democrat Printing Company, 1914.

Fant, Henry A. *Arthur MacArthur and the Philippine Insurrection.* Unpublished M.A. Thesis, Mississippi State University, 1963.

Fitch, Michael Hendrick. *The Chattanooga Campaign.* Madison: Wisconsin History Commission, 1911.

Ganoe, William Addleman. *The History of the United States Army.* Ashton, Maryland: Eric Lundberg, 1964.

Gatewood, Willard B., Jr. *Black Americans and the White Man's Burden 1898-1903.* Urbana, IL: University of Illinois Press, 1975.

Gregory, John C. *History of Milwaukee, Vol. II.* Chicago: S.J. Clarke Publishing Company, 1931.

Harris, Brayton. *The Age of the Battleship, 1890-1922.* New York: Franklin Watts, Inc., 1965.

History of Milwaukee. Vol. I. Chicago: The Western Historical Company, 1881.

Holmes, Fred L., Ed. *Wisconsin: Stability, Progress, Beauty.* Vol. II. Chicago: Lewis Publishing Company, 1946.

James, D. Clayton. *The Years of MacArthur, Vol. I, 1880-1941.* Boston: Houghton Mifflin Company, 1970.

Langer, William L., Ed. *An Encyclopedia of World History.* Boston: Houghton Mifflin Company, 1948.

Lee, Clark and Richard Henschel. *Douglas MacArthur.* New York: Henry Holt and Company, 1952.

Leech, Margaret. *In the Days of McKinley.* New York: Harper and Brothers Publishers, 1959.

MacArthur Memorial Week: June 8-14, 1979, Milwaukee, Wisconsin. Milwaukee County Historical Society, 1979.

The MacArthurs of Milwaukee. Milwaukee: Milwaukee County Historical Society, 1979.

Mahajani, Usha. *Philippine Nationalism: External Challenge and Filipino Response, 1565-1946.* St. Lucia: University of Queensland Press, 1971.

Manchester, William. *American Caesar: Douglas MacArthur, 1880-1965*. Boston: Little, Brown and Company, 1978.

Mann, Conklin. "Some Ancestoral Lines of General Douglas MacArthur," pp. 170-172 in *New York Genealogical and Biographical Record*, 73 (July, 1942).

Miller, Stuart Creighton. *Benevolent Assimilation: The American Conquest of the Philippines, 1899-1903*. New Haven: Yale University Press, 1982.

Minger, Ralph E. "Taft, MacArthur, and the Establishment of Civil Government in the Philippines," pp. 303-331 in *The Ohio Historical Quarterly*, 70 (1961).

Mitchell, Joseph. *Decisive Battles of the Civil War*. New York: Ballantine Books, 1983.

Muggah, Mary Gates and Paul H. Raihle. *The MacArthur Story*. Chippewa Falls, WI: Chippewa Falls Book Agency, 1945.

Nesbit, Robert C. *Wisconsin: A History*. Madison: University of Wisconsin Press, 1973.

Petillo, Carol Morris. *Douglas MacArthur: The Philippine Years*. Ph.D. Dissertation, Rutgers, The State University of New Jersey, 1979.

Petillo, Carol Morris. *Douglas MacArthur: The Philippine Years*. Bloomington, IN: Indiana University Press, 1981.

Pomeroy, William J. *American Neo-Colonialism: Its Emergence in the Philippines and Asia*. New York: International Publishers Co., Inc., 1970.

Ridlon, G.T., Sr. *Saco Valley Settlements and Families*. Portland, ME: Lakeside Press, 1895.

Specter, Ronald. *Admiral of the New Empire: The Life and Career of George Dewey*. Baton Rouge: Louisiana State University Press, 1974.

Stanley, Peter W. *A Nation in the Making: The Philippines and the United States, 1899-1921*. Cambridge: Harvard University Press, 1974.

Steinberg, David Joel, Ed. *In Search of Southeast Asia: A Modern History*. Honolulu: University of Hawaii Press, 1985.

Stratemeyer, Edward. *Under MacArthur in Luzon*. Boston: Lee and Shepard Publishers, 1901.

Thompson, E. Bruce. *Matthew Hale Carpenter: Webster of the West*. Madison: The State Historical Society of Wisconsin, 1954.

Trask, David F. *The War with Spain in 1898*. New York: MacMillan Publishing Company, 1981.

Usher, Ellis Baker. *Wisconsin: Its Story and Biography, 1848-1913 Vol. VII*. New York: Lewis Publishing Company, 1913.

Vandiver, Frank E. *Black Jack: The Life and Times of John J. Pershing*. 2 Vols. College Station: Texas A&M University Press, 1977.

Watrous, Major J.A. "How the Boy Won: General MacArthur's First Victory," pp. 770-771 in *Saturday Evening Post*, 172 (February 24, 1900).

Welch, Richard E., Jr. *Response to Imperialism: The United States and the Philippine-American War, 1899-1902*. Chapel Hill: University of North Carolina Press, 1979.

Wells, Robert W. *Wisconsin in the Civil War*. Milwaukee: The Milwaukee Journal, 1964.

Wells, Robert W. *Yesterday's Milwaukee*. Miami, FL: E.A. Seemann Publishing Inc., 1976.

Wolff, Leon. *Little Brown Brother: How the United States Purchased and Pacified the Philippine Islands at the Century's Turn*. Garden City, NY: Doubleday and Company, Inc., 1961.

Worchester, Dean C. *The Philippines Past and Present*. 2 Vols. New York: The MacMillan Company, 1930.

Young, James Rankin and J. Hampton Moore, *History of Our War with Spain*. Library of Congress, N.d.

Young, Kenneth Ray. *The General's General: The Life and Times of Arthur MacArthur*. Boulder: Westview Press, 1994.

Zornow, William F. "Funston Captures Aguinaldo," pp. 24-29, 107 in *American Heritage*, 9 (February, 1958).

Index

HISTRIA
BOOKS

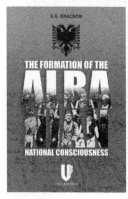